Maths Out Loud
Year 3

by
Phil McErlain

BEAM

Acknowledgements

Jane Prothero and Woodlands Primary School, Leeds

Karen Holman and Paddox Primary School, Rugby

Heather Nixon and Gayhurst Primary School, Buckinghamshire

John Ellard and Kingsley Primary School, Northampton

Jackie Smith, Catherine Torr and Roberttown CE J & I School, Kirklees

Wendy Price and St Martin's CE Primary School, Wolverhampton

Helen Elis Jones, University of Wales, Bangor

Ruth Trundley, Devon Curriculum Services, Exeter

Trudy Lines and Bibury CE Primary School, Gloucestershire

Elaine Folen and St Paul's Infant School, Surrey

Jane Airey and Frith Manor Primary School, Barnet

Beverley Godfrey, South Wales Home Educators' Network

Kay Brunsdon and Gwyrosydd Infant School, Swansea

Keith Cadman, Wolverhampton Advisory Services

Helen Andrews and Blue Coat School, Birmingham

Oakridge Parochial School, Gloucestershire

The Islington BEAM Development Group

Published by BEAM Education
Maze Workshops
72a Southgate Road
London N1 3JT
Telephone 020 7684 3323
Fax 020 7684 3334
Email info@beam.co.uk
www.beam.co.uk
© Beam Education 2006
ISBN 1 903142 85 7
British Library Cataloguing-in-Publication Data
Data available
Edited by Marion Dill
Designed by Malena Wilson-Max
Photographs by Len Cross
Thanks to Rotherfield Primary School
Printed in England by Cromwell Press Ltd

Contents

Introduction

Language plays an important part in the learning of mathematics – especially oral language. Children's relationship to the subject, their grasp of it and sense of ownership all depend on discussion and interaction – as do the social relationships that provide the context for learning. A classroom where children talk about mathematics is one that will help build their confidence and transform their whole attitude to learning.

Why is speaking and listening important in maths?

- Talking is creative. In expressing thoughts and discussing ideas, children actually shape these ideas, make connections and hone their definitions of what words mean.
- You cannot teach what a word means – you can only introduce it, explain it, then let children try it out, misuse it, see when it works and how it fits with what they already know and, eventually, make it their own.
- Speaking and listening to other children involves and motivates children – they are more likely to learn and remember than when engaging silently with a textbook or worksheet.
- As you listen to children, you identify children's misconceptions and realise which connections (between bits of maths) they have not yet made.

How does this book help me include 'speaking and listening' in maths?

- The lessons are structured to use and develop oral language skills in mathematics. Each lesson uses one or more classroom techniques that foster the use of spoken language and listening skills.
- The grid on p17 shows those speaking and listening objectives that are suitable for developing through the medium of mathematics. Each lesson addresses one of these objectives.
- The lessons draw on a bank of classroom techniques which are described on p8. These techniques are designed to promote children's use of speaking and listening in a variety of ways.

How does 'using and applying mathematics' fit in with these lessons?

- Many of the mathematical activities in this book involve problem solving, communication and reasoning, all key areas of 'using and applying mathematics' (U&A). Where this aspect of a lesson is particularly significant, this is acknowledged and expanded on in one of the 'asides' to the main lesson.

What about children with particular needs?

- For children who have impaired hearing, communication is particularly important, as it is all too easy for them to become isolated from their peers. Speaking and listening activities, even if adapted, simplified or supported by an assistant, help such children be a part of their learning community and to participate in the curriculum on offer.

- Children who speak English as an additional language benefit from speaking and listening activities, especially where these are accompanied by diagrams, drawings or the manipulation of numbers or shapes, which help give meaning to the language. Check that they understand the key words needed for the topic being discussed and, where possible, model the activity, paying particular attention to the use of these key words. Remember to build in time for thinking and reflecting on oral work.

- Differences in children's backgrounds affect the way they speak to their peers and adults. The lessons in this book can help children acquire a rich repertoire of ways to interact and work with others. Children who are less confident with written forms can develop confidence through speaking and listening.

- Gender can be an issue in acquiring and using speaking and listening skills. Girls may be collaborative and tentative, while boys sometimes can be more assertive about expressing their ideas. Address such differences by planning different groups, partners, classroom seating and activities. These lessons build on children's strengths and challenge them in areas where they are less strong.

What are the 'personal skills' learning objectives?

- There is a range of personal and social skills that children need to develop across the curriculum and throughout their school career. These include enquiry skills, creative thinking skills and ways of working with others. Some are particularly relevant to the maths classroom, and these are listed on the grid on p18.

What about assessment?

- Each lesson concludes with a section called 'Assessment for learning', which offers suggestions for what to look out for during the lesson and questions to ask in order to assess children's learning of all three learning objectives. There is also help on what may lie behind children's failure to meet these objectives and suggestions for teaching that might rectify the situation.

- Each section of four lessons includes a sheet of self-assessment statements to be printed from the accompanying CD-ROM and to be filled in at the end of each lesson or when all four are completed. Display the sheet and also give children their own copies. Then go through the statements, discussing and interpreting them as necessary. Ask children to complete their self-assessments with a partner they frequently work with. They should each fill in their own sheet, then look at it with their partner who adds their own viewpoint.

How can I make the best use of these lessons?

- Aim to develop a supportive classroom climate, where all ideas are accepted and considered, even if they may seem strange or incorrect. You will need to model this yourself in order for children to see what acceptance and open-mindedness look like.
- Create an ethos of challenge, where children are required to think about puzzles and questions.
- Slow down. Don't expect answers straight away when you ask questions. Build in thinking time where you do not communicate with the children, so that they have to reflect on their answers before making them. Expect quality rather than quantity.
- Model the language of discussion. Children who may be used to maths being either 'correct' or 'incorrect' need to learn by example what debate means. Choose a debating partner from the class, or work with another adult, and demonstrate uncertainty, challenge, exploration, questioning …
- Tell children what they will be learning in the lesson. Each lesson concludes with an 'Assessment for learning' section offering suggestions for what to look out for to assess children's learning of all three learning objectives. Share these with the children at the start of the lesson to involve them in their own learning process.

How should I get the best out of different groupings?

- Get children used to working in a range of different groupings: pairs, threes or fours or as a whole class.
- Organise pairs in different ways on different occasions: familiar maths partners (who can communicate well); pairs of friends (who enjoy working together); children of differing abilities (who can learn something from each other); someone they don't know (to get them used to talking and listening respectfully to any other person).
- Give children working in pairs and groups some time for independent thought and work.
- Support pairs when they prepare to report back to the class. Go over with them what they have done or discovered and what they might say about this. Help them make brief notes – just single words or phrases – to remind them what they are going to say. If you are busy, ask an assistant or another child to take over your role. Then, when it comes to feedback time, support them by gentle probes or questions: "What did you do next?" or "What do your notes say?"

Classroom techniques used in this book

Ways of working

Peer tutoring
pairs of children

good for

This technique can benefit both the child who is being 'taught' and also the 'tutor' who develops a clearer understanding of what they themselves have learned and, in explaining it, can make new connections and solidify old ones. Children often make the best teachers, because they are close to the state of not knowing and can remember what helped them bridge the gap towards understanding.

how to organise it

'Peer tutoring' can work informally – children work in mixed ability pairs, and if one child understands an aspect of the work that the other doesn't, they work together in a tutor/pupil relationship to make sure the understanding is shared by both. Alternatively, you can structure it more formally. Observe children at work and identify those who are confident and accurate with the current piece of mathematics. Give them the title of 'Expert' and ask them to work with individuals needing support. Don't overuse this: the tutor has a right to work and learn at their own level, and tutoring others should only play a small part in their school lives.

Talking partners
pairs of children

good for

This technique helps children develop and practise the skills of collaboration in an unstructured way. Children can articulate their thinking, listen to one another and support each other's learning in a 'safe' situation.

how to organise it

Pairs who have previously worked together (for example, 'One between two', below) work together informally. The children in these pairs have had time to build up trust between them, and should have the confidence to tackle a new, less structured task. If you regularly use 'Talking partners', pairs of children will get used to working together. This helps them develop confidence, but runs the risk that children mutually reinforce their misunderstandings. In this case, changing partners occasionally can bring fresh life to the class by creating new meetings of minds.

One between two
pairs of children

good for

This technique helps children develop their skills of explaining, questioning and listening – behaviours that are linked to positive learning outcomes. Use it when the children have two or more problems or calculations to solve.

how to organise it

Pairs share a pencil (or calculator or other tool), and each assumes one of two roles: 'Solver' or 'Recorder'. (Supplying just one pencil encourages children to stay in role by preventing the Solver from making their own notes.)

The Solver has a problem and works through it out loud. The Recorder keeps a written record of what the Solver is doing. If the Solver needs something written down or a calculation done on the calculator, they must ask the Recorder to do this for them. If the Recorder is not sure of what the Solver is doing, they ask for further explanations, but do not engage in actually solving the problem. After each problem, children swap roles.

Introduce this way of working by modelling it yourself with a confident child partner: you talk through your own method of solving a problem, and the child records this thought process on the board.

Barrier games/Telephone conversations

pairs of children

good for

These techniques help children focus on spoken language rather than gesture or facial expression. The children must listen carefully to what is said, because they cannot see the person speaking.

how to organise it

Barrier games focus on giving and receiving instructions. Pairs of children work with a book or screen between them, so that they cannot see each other's work. The speaker gives information or instructions to the listener. The listener, in turn, asks questions to clarify understanding and gain information.

In 'Telephone conversations', the technique is taken further, as children sit back to back, with only imaginary 'telephones' for conversation.

Rotating roles

groups of various sizes

good for

Working in a small group to solve a problem encourages children to articulate their thinking and support each other's learning.

how to organise it

Careful structuring discourages individuals from taking the lead too often. Assign different roles to the children in the group: Chairperson, Reader, Recorder, Questioner, and so on. Over time, everyone has a turn at each role. You may wish to give children 'role labels' to remind them of their current role.

When you introduce this technique, model the role of chairperson in a group, with the rest of the class watching. Show how to include everyone and then discuss with the children what you have done, so as to make explicit techniques that they can use.

Discussion

Think, pair, share
groups of four

good for

Putting pairs together to work as a group of four helps avoid the situation where children in pairs mutually reinforce their common misunderstandings. It gives children time to think on their own, rehearse their thoughts with a partner and then discuss in a larger group. This encourages everyone to join in and discourages the 'quick thinkers' from dominating a discussion.

how to organise it

The technique is a development of 'Tell your partner' and involves the following:
- One or two minutes for individuals to think about a problem or statement and, possibly, to jot down their initial thoughts
- Two or three minutes where individuals work in pairs to share their thoughts
- Four or five minutes for two pairs to join together and discuss
- If you wish, you can also allow ten minutes for reporting back from some or all groups and whole-class discussion.

You can vary this pattern and the timings, but always aim to give children some 'private' thinking time.

Talking stick
any number of children

good for

Giving all children a turn at speaking and being listened to.

how to organise it

Provide the class with decorated sticks, which confer status on whoever holds them. Then, in a small or large group (or even the whole class), make it the rule that only the person holding the stick may speak, while the other children listen. You can use the stick in various ways: pass it around the circle; tell the child with the stick to pass it to whoever they want to speak next; have a chairperson who decides who will hold the stick next; ask the person with the stick to repeat what the previous person said before adding their own comments or ideas.

Tell your partner
pairs

good for

Whole-class question-and-answer sessions favour the quick and the confident and do not provide time and space for slower thinkers. This technique involves all children in answering questions and in discussion.

how to organise it

Do this in one of two ways:

- When you have just asked a question or presented an idea to think about, ask each child to turn to their neighbour or partner and tell them the answer. They then take turns to speak and to listen.
- Work less formally, simply asking children to talk over their ideas with a partner. Children may find this sharing difficult at first. They may not value talking to another child, preferring to talk to the teacher or not expressing their ideas at all. In this case, do some work on listening skills such as timing 'a minute each way' or repeating back to their partner what they have just said.

Devil's advocate

any number of children

good for

Statements – false or ambiguous as well as true – are often better than questions at provoking discussion.

how to organise it

In discussion with children, take the role of 'Devil's advocate', in which you make statements for them to agree or disagree with and to argue about.

To avoid confusing children by making false statements yourself, mention 'a friend' or 'someone you know' who makes these statements (a version of the 'silly teddy' who, in Nursery and Reception, makes mistakes for the children to correct). Alternatively, explain that when you make statements with your hands behind your back, your fingers may be crossed and you may be saying things that are not true.

Reporting back

Ticket to explain

individuals

good for

This is a way of structuring feedback which helps children get the maximum out of offering explanations to the class. Everyone hears a method explained twice, and children have to listen carefully to their peers, rather than simply think about their own method.

how to organise it

When individuals want to explain their method of working to the class, their 'ticket' to be able to do this is to re-explain the method demonstrated by the child immediately before them. Or children work with a partner and explain their ideas to each other. When called on to speak, they explain their partner's idea and then their own.

Heads or tails
pairs of children

good for

When pairs of children work together, one child may rely heavily on the other to make decisions and to communicate or one child may take over, despite the efforts of the other child to have a say. This technique encourages pairs to work together to understand something and helps prevent an uneven workload.

how to organise it

Invite pairs to the front of the class to explain their ideas or solutions. When they get to the front, ask them to nominate who is heads and who is tails, then toss a coin to decide which of them does the talking. They have one opportunity to 'ask a friend' (probably their partner). As all children in the class know that they may be chosen to speak in this way, because the toss of the coin could make either of them into the 'explainer', they are motivated to work with their partner to reach a common understanding. Assigning the choice of explainer to the toss of a coin stops children feeling that anyone is picking on them personally (do warn them in advance, though!). Variation: If a pair of children has different ideas on a topic, ask both to offer explanations of each other's ideas.

1, 2, 3, 4
groups of four

good for

This technique offers the same benefits as 'Heads or tails', but is used for groups of four children rather than pairs.

how to organise it

This is a technique identical to 'Heads or tails', but with groups of four. Instead of tossing a coin, children are numbered 1 to 4, and the speaker is chosen by the roll of a dice (if 5 or 6 come up, simply roll again).

Additional techniques

Below are some further classroom techniques that are referred to in the lessons in this book.

Chewing the fat
any number of children

good for

Leaving ideas or questions unresolved provides thoughtful children with the opportunity to extend their thinking. Many mathematicians like to have problems to think about, just as some people like crossword clues to occupy their mind.

how to organise it

Sometimes end a lesson with ideas, problems or challenges for children to ponder in their own time as you may have run out of time or one of the children has come up with a question or an idea which can only be discussed the next day.

Reframing
any number of children

good for

'Reframing' alters the meaning of something by altering its context or description. It helps children find their way into a difficult or new idea by hearing it rephrased and enlarged.

how to organise it

Rephrase children's words using a variety of language: "You read that out as 'twenty-five multiplied by seven'. That means seven lots of 25." After a few seconds, say: "Imagine a pile of 25 beans, and you've got seven piles like that."

Goldfish bowl
whole class

good for

This technique enables you to demonstrate a new game or activity to any number of children in a practical and accessible way and to deal with children's queries and misunderstandings as they arise.

how to organise it

Ask the class to stand or sit in a circle around one pair or group of children and to watch as they follow your instructions to demonstrate a game or activity. You can adapt this technique in various ways. For example, children who want to suggest a move to a player can stand behind them and put a hand on their shoulder to indicate that they have a suggestion to make. Alternatively, you can stop the game at any time and discuss with the observers what is happening, asking for their comments and suggestions.

Charts

Classroom techniques

This chart shows which of the classroom techniques previously described are used in which lessons.

	NUMBERS AND THE NUMBER SYSTEM	FRACTIONS, DECIMALS, PERCENTAGES, RATIO AND PROPORTION	ADDITION AND SUBTRACTION	MULTIPLICATION AND DIVISION	HANDLING DATA	MEASURES	SHAPE AND SPACE
	Lesson	Lesson	Lesson	Lesson	Lesson	Lesson	Lesson
One between two	4	5, 7		13, 16	20		
Talking partners			11	15			28
Rotating roles	1	8	9		17	24	
Peer tutoring			10	14		22	
Barrier games / Telephone conversations							25 to 27
Tell your partner	3					23	
Devil's advocate		6			19		
Think, pair, share	2					21	
Ticket to explain					18		
Heads or tails / 1, 2, 3, 4			12				

Speaking and listening skills

This chart shows which speaking and listening skills are practised in which lessons.

	NUMBERS AND THE NUMBER SYSTEM	FRACTIONS, DECIMALS, PERCENTAGES, RATIO AND PROPORTION	ADDITION AND SUBTRACTION	MULTIPLICATION AND DIVISION	HANDLING DATA	MEASURES	SHAPE AND SPACE
	Lesson	Lesson	Lesson	Lesson	Lesson	Lesson	Lesson
Explain and justify thinking	1, 2	8		13, 16	20	21	
Use precise language to explain ideas or give information		5, 7				24	25
Share and discuss ideas and reach consensus			10			22	
Reach a common understanding with a partner			11	14		23	28
Contribute to small-group and whole-class discussion		6	12	15	17		
Listen and follow instructions accurately	4						27
Listen with sustained concentration	3		9		18, 19		26

Personal skills

This chart shows which personal skills are practised in which lessons.

	NUMBERS AND THE NUMBER SYSTEM	FRACTIONS, DECIMALS, PERCENTAGES, RATIO AND PROPORTION	ADDITION AND SUBTRACTION	MULTIPLICATION AND DIVISION	HANDLING DATA	MEASURES	SHAPE AND SPACE
	Lesson	Lesson	Lesson	Lesson	Lesson	Lesson	Lesson
Organise work							
Plan ways to solve a problem			9		20		
Plan and manage a group task		6, 8				21	
Use different approaches to tackle a problem				15			
Organise findings	1						
Work with others							
Discuss and agree ways of working					17		
Work cooperatively with others	2	7		16	19		28
Overcome difficulties and recover from mistakes			10			23	25
Show awareness and understanding of others' needs	4						26
Give feedback sensitively				13			
Improve learning and performance							
Reflect on learning			12		18		
Critically evaluate own work							27
Assess learning progress			11			22	
Take pride in work				14		24	
Develop confidence in own judgements	3	5					

Lessons

Numbers and the number system

Lesson 1
Number properties

Lesson 2
Ordering numbers

Lesson 3
Estimating quantities

Lesson 4
Adding 1 or 10

Learning objectives

	Lessons			
	1	**2**	**3**	**4**
Maths objectives				
recognise a range of number properties	●			
understand place value		●		
make sensible estimates			●	
say the number that is 1 or 10 more or less than a two-digit number				●
Speaking and listening skills				
explain and justify thinking	●	●		
listen with sustained concentration			●	
listen and follow instructions accurately				●
Personal skills				
organise work: organise findings	●			
work with others: work cooperatively with others		●		
improve learning and performance: develop confidence in own judgements			●	
work with others: show awareness and understanding of others' needs				●

About these lessons

Lesson 1: Number properties

(m) Recognise a range of number properties

Children in Year 3 should be learning the mathematical ideas of odd, even and multiple as well as learning to recognise multiples of 2, 5 and 10. This activity encourages children to use these ideas as they seek to eliminate numbers to find the mystery number.

Explain and justify thinking

Classroom technique: Rotating roles

Taking turns to answer and ask the questions and to work out the implications of the answers ensures that all children get an opportunity to think and to put that thinking into words.

Organise work: organise findings

Children record the deductions they have made from a particular piece of information on a number grid. For example, if the answer to "Is the mystery number less than 30?" is "Yes", then they cross out numbers 30 and above. This structure helps children develop systematic working and recording.

Lesson 2: Ordering numbers

(m) Understand place value

An understanding of place value is fundamentally important in the development of children's understanding of number. In this lesson, children play a game arranging digits, aiming to make a higher three-digit number than the other team.

Explain and justify thinking

Classroom technique: Think, pair, share

In the plenary, children think briefly about where to place a number in order to win the point. They then turn to their partner and explain their ideas before discussing the matter as a group of four.

Work with others: work cooperatively with others

Children play in teams of two, working together to get a higher score than the other team.

Lesson 3: Estimating quantities

(m) Make sensible estimates

Children only gradually develop the ability to estimate and need the opportunity, and the confidence, to experiment, to make mistakes and to learn from them. In this lesson, they make several estimates involving collections of over 100 and explore the methods used for making these estimates.

Listen with sustained concentration

Classroom technique: Tell your partner

Children listen to an explanation given by their partner, or another child, and then repeat it back to them. This encourages children to listen with concentration to what is said.

Improve learning and performance: develop confidence in own judgements

Focusing on methods gives children a valuable tool to use in estimating the quantities and helps them develop confidence in their abilities in this area.

Lesson 4: Adding 1 or 10

(m) Say the number that is 1 or 10 more or less than a two-digit number

On a 100-grid, each number is 1 more than the one to its left and one less than the one to its right, 10 more than the one above it and 10 less than the one below. This makes the 100-grid an excellent tool to use in practising adding and subtracting 1 and 10 to and from a two-digit number.

Listen and follow instructions accurately

Classroom technique: One between two

One child makes the decisions and instructs their partner what to write, and where. The child writing must listen carefully to their partner's instructions and ask for more information as necessary.

Work with others: show awareness and understanding of others' needs

When working in pairs, taking on the role of tutor and telling the other child what to write requires sensitivity and the willingness to think about what information that child needs.

Number properties
Classroom technique: Rotating roles

Learning objectives

m **Maths**
Recognise a range of number properties

Speaking and listening
'Explain what you think and why you think it'
Explain and justify thinking

Personal skills
'Organise your results'
Organise work: organise findings

w **Words and phrases**
multiple, odd, even, more, larger, bigger, greater, less, smaller, compare, work out, solve, check

r **Resources**
display copies of RS1 and RS2
for each group:
three copies of RS1
three sets of question slips cut from RS2
10 or more different-coloured pens or pencils
100-grid (optional)

Filling in the blanks
Discuss how to do this: "Is the mystery number less than ...? How shall we fill in that blank? Would 25 be a good number to put there?"

Working systematically
This is an opportunity to model systematic working: going through the numbers or rows in order and making sure to cross out all relevant numbers.

Multiples
Some children may find it easier to think about 'in the ... times table' rather than 'is a multiple of'. However, encourage children to use and become familiar with the more general term 'multiple'.

Different colours
Using different colours allows the children to check the deductions they have made from a particular piece of information. If the question slip "Is the mystery number less than 30?" has a 'yes' written in red, then the numbers 30 and more should be crossed out in red, but none of the numbers below 30.

Explain and justify thinking
Ask questions which will require the children to put their thinking into words: "The answer to that question is 'No'. Tell me how you work out what numbers you can cross out."

Introduction

Display RS1 and some of the questions from RS2. Read out the questions with the class.

One child writes a mystery number between 1 and 49 on a piece of paper and keeps it hidden. Another child chooses a question from those displayed and reads it to the child with the mystery number. Help that child work out the answer and reply with a 'yes' or 'no'.

Ask which numbers can be crossed out on the first grid on RS1 as a result of the answer given. Continue like this, showing more questions from RS2 as appropriate.

The answer to "Does the mystery number end in 0?" was "No". So which numbers can we cross out?

Do you need to go through all the numbers in turn and check if you can cross them out?

Groups of three

Each group works with three copies of RS1 and a set of question slips cut from RS2, for each 'turn' (three sets in all).

Child A writes down a mystery number and keeps it hidden. They then sit facing away from the other two children, with the second grid for reference.

Child B picks a question from the set (if it is one with a blank, they fill in the blank) and asks Child A the question.

Child B writes the answer in colour on the question slip, discusses with Child C which numbers on the first grid to cross out and does so, using the same colour.

Child B and C swap roles and continue, using a different colour each time until they discover the mystery number.

Children then rotate roles.

How many questions did you use to get that mystery number? Which is the quickest one you've done?

How did you work out that you could cross out those numbers?

Are those all the numbers you can cross out for that answer? Could there be any more?

Support: Use the first four lines (up to 28) of a grid and the first twelve question slips from RS2.

Extend: Use a 100-grid, allowing children to choose a question slip rather than picking one at random. Alternatively, children write their own question slips.

Plenary

Choose a mystery number yourself. Ask the class for two identifying questions and write these up. Answer them and show in colour how each answer eliminates different numbers.

> The answer to "Does it have a 1 in it?" is "No".
> So cross out in yellow: 10, 11, 12, …
>
> The answer to "Is it in the 3 times table?" is also "No". So cross out in green: 3, 6, 9, 12, …

Discuss which question provided the most information.

What are the multiples of 5? How do you recognise them?

What would be a useful question you could ask to find my number?

Assessment for learning

Can the children	**If not**
Accurately interpret the answers to questions about 'greater than/less than'? About multiples?	Work with children on different number grids if they need clarification on the meaning of the terms in question. Mark numbers that are more than 25 or multiples of 3, and so on, sometimes making deliberate errors for children to spot.
Explain how they know which set of numbers to cross out?	Go through the numbers on the grid one by one, asking "Shall we cross out this number?" Help children put into words the reason why, or why not.
Record their findings systematically?	Model organised working yourself, doing the same kind of activity on another occasion. Ask children who do work methodically to work with less orderly partners, acting as 'peer tutors' (p8).

Ordering numbers

Classroom technique: Think, pair, share

Learning objectives

m Maths
Understand place value

Speaking and listening
'Explain what you think and why you think it'
Explain and justify thinking

Personal skills
'Work cooperatively with others'
Work with others: work cooperatively with others

W Words and phrases
units, ones, tens, hundreds, digit, one-, two- or three-digit number, compare, order, size, explain, convince

r Resources
display copy of RS3
for each group:
two copies of RS3
0–9 dice
place value arrow cards (optional)
100-grid (optional)

Skills
The skill of the game lies in deciding which box to use for the first and second rolls of the dice.

Think, pair, share
Children briefly think about where the number should go before turning to their partner and sharing their thoughts.

Place value
Keep a note of any children who seem to be struggling with place value in order to give them extra help as soon as possible.

Introduction

Display RS3. Demonstrate the game by playing against the class.

Each player has one set of three boxes. Players take turns to roll a 0–9 dice, each time choosing which box to write the digit in. The aim is to make a higher three-digit number than the other player – whichever player does so gets one point.

Remind children that the first digit in a three-digit number is worth hundreds, the second is worth tens and the third box is worth ones.

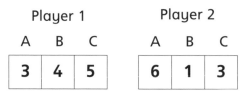

Player 2 wins.

m *We have a 0. Shall we put it in box A, box B or box C?*

Speaking and listening *You have rolled a 5. Talk with your partner about which box to put it in, and why.*

Pairs

Pairs of children work with two copies of RS3. They play the game ten times, keeping a record of the points scored, and discuss who is the winner.

Ask various pairs about their reasons for choosing particular boxes.

m *Which are the best numbers to get? Which are the worst numbers?*

Speaking and listening *Which numbers are most difficult to decide about?*

Speaking and listening *What do you usually do when you get a zero? Why?*

Personal skills *What can you do so that your partner enjoys working with you?*

Support: Use two boxes instead of three. Model the numbers children
make with place value arrow cards and help them find these numbers
on a 100-grid.

Extend: Use four or more boxes.

Plenary

Play six or eight rounds of the game against the class, rolling the dice for
your own and the class's turns and modelling good reasoning – for example,
"That 3 is not worth much, so I'll put it in the ones box"; "That 7 would be
worth 7 hundreds if I put it in this box."

Encourage discussion about strategies for placing numbers on the first
and second turns and ask children to explain which boxes they choose,
and why.

Focus of discussion
In this part of the lesson, each
group is working with the same
numbers. This makes it possible
to emphasise the reasoning
behind the decisions made.

Why is it best to place a high number in the hundreds box?

Why do you think you lost that round?

Did all of your group agree about what to do?

Assessment for learning

Can the children

Ⓜ Recognise which of two three-digit numbers
is the higher?

Explain why they chose a particular box
for a digit?

Share the work with their partner?

If not

Ⓜ Model hundreds, tens and ones with cubes,
counters or base-ten blocks so that children
have a visual image of the size and value of
100, 10 and 1.

Invite a confident child to explain to the class why
they would choose certain boxes for a digit, then
ask other children to repeat this explanation to
each other.

Talk with the children about what 'working
cooperatively' means. Make sure to praise children
who work well together, achieving the task they
were set.

Estimating quantities

Classroom technique: Tell your partner

Learning objectives

m Maths
Make sensible estimates

Speaking and listening
'Listen well'
Listen with sustained
concentration

Personal skills
'Develop confidence
about what you think
and decide'
Improve learning and
performance: develop
confidence in own judgements

w Words and phrases
guess, estimate,
nearly, roughly, close to,
approximately, count, check,
explain, reason, method

r Resources
large jar containing
between 100 and 1000
marbles
other collections of objects
for each pair:
wipe boards

Develop confidence

Children's confidence can be
dented easily at this stage,
so treat any offering that they
make seriously, even 'a million'.

Estimating

Estimating generally involves
multiplying in some way, and
many children of this age
have only limited ideas of
multiplication. Take this
opportunity to talk about
repeated sets of the same size
to help children develop their
understanding. You could model
this by organising the marbles
into groups of much the same
size, but not counting them all.

Tell your partner

Children repeat their partner's
explanation back to them as
soon as they have heard it and
check for clarification if there is
anything they don't understand.

Introduction

Display a large jar containing between 100 and 1000
marbles. Remind children that there is a difference
between an estimate and a guess: there is reasoning
involved in an estimate, whereas a guess is just a
guess. Ask three children for estimates of the number
of marbles and an explanation of their thinking. If it
turns out that an estimate is only a guess, accept that
without criticism at this stage, but make sure you get
at least a couple of reasoned explanations.

Scribe the estimates. Working in pairs, children write
them in order on their wipe boards, then write down
their own estimate as well, with a line showing where
it would come in the order.

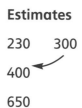

Estimates

230   300

400

650

Organise the counting of the marbles in tens and in
tens of tens to reinforce ideas of place value.

Compare the result with the ordered list of estimates
and ask for any explanations or comments.

m *How much room would 50 marbles take up?
Do you think they would fill the whole jar?*

*Jasmine counted the layers of marbles in the jar.
She thought there were maybe 10 marbles in each
layer and counted up in tens. Can you describe that
method to your partner?*

*Notice whether your estimate was too low or too
high and see if that helps you with the estimating
you do next.*

Pairs

Display two different collections of objects, divide the
class into two and allocate one collection to each half.

Children write down an estimate for their collection
and share their answer with their partner, explaining
their thinking.

They discuss and agree one of their two estimates or choose a new one.

Repeat this with the two collections swapped, so that each pair ends up with an estimate for each collection.

(m) *How many counters would fit in half the jar? Can you double that?*

(🗣) *Do you agree with what your partner just said? Can you repeat it in your own words?*

(☺) *Are you feeling more confident about estimating now?*

Support: Provide a collection of 20 to 100 objects.

Extend: Tell children you expect a close, well-reasoned estimate.

Collections of objects

Over 100:
– large jar of acorns, cubes, beads, building bricks, buttons, 1p pieces, counters
– words in a magazine article, newspaper column or page (chosen carefully)
– pencils and pens, pasta shapes in a bag

20–100:
– large jar of conkers, marbles, wooden cubes, beads

Develop confidence

Remind children that estimating is all about approximation – accuracy is neither expected nor necessary. Emphasise that practice such as this helps children develop their skills.

Plenary

Collect estimates and brief justifications for the two collections. Put these in order, with the children's help.

Count the sets of objects, using the same techniques as in the introduction, and ask for comments or explanations.

(m) *Could there be as many as 10 000 acorns? Tell your partner what you think.*

(☺) *There are 345 acorns. Anyone who estimated between 300 and 400 acorns has done really well.*

Assessment for learning

Can the children

(m) Make a reasonable estimate of the number of objects in a jar?

(🗣) Repeat back to you what another child has just said about their estimate?

(☺) Speak confidently when telling you their estimate?

If not

(m) Do more estimating work in pairs, using smaller quantities of objects.

(🗣) Ask the child to repeat back an explanation broken into chunks: "First, Faran counted 10 marbles and saw how much space they took up ..."

(☺) Consider whether children need to work at a simpler level. Observe children working with their partner and see if they appear more confident talking to a peer than to an adult.

Adding 1 or 10

Classroom technique: One between two

Learning objectives

Ⓜ Maths
Say the number that is 1 or 10 more or less than a two-digit number

Speaking and listening
'Listen and follow instructions'
Listen and follow instructions accurately

Personal skills
'Think about what other people need'
Work with others: show awareness and understanding of others' needs

Ⓦ Words and phrases
units, ones, tens, digit, two-digit number, place, place value, one more, ten more, one less, ten less

ⓡ Resources
display 100-grid
for each pair:
copy of RS4
100-grids

Tell your partner
Using this technique (p10), children share with their neighbour what they know about the arrangement of numbers on the grid.

The structure of the 100-grid
Remind children that each number is 1 more than the one to its left and one less than the one to its right, 10 more than the one above it and 10 less than the one below. In the next part of the lesson, they will have an opportunity to apply and develop this understanding.

Solving the problems
The problems get gradually harder and, by the end, involve not only the four possibilities in the introduction – add 1, subtract 1, add 10, subtract 10 – but also combinations of some of them – add 9, subtract 9, add 11, subtract 11.

Introduction

Display a 100-grid and talk about how the numbers are arranged.

Draw a horizontal row of four boxes and explain that this is part of a 100-grid. Ask for a number between 3 and 99, not ending in 0, 1 or 2, and write the number in the third box.

Ask for suggestions for the other three numbers and explanations as to how they were worked out. Repeat this with a vertical column of four boxes, using a starting number between 21 and 90 and putting it in the third box down.

Ⓜ *Tell me what number I should write here.*

Ⓜ *How do the numbers in the columns increase?*

Pairs

Each pair of children works with a copy of RS4. Using 'One between two' (p8), Child A makes the decisions, while Child B has the pencil. Starting with problem 1, Child A chooses a number that satisfies the conditions given and asks Child B to write it in the shaded box.

Child A then chooses an empty box and tells Child B how to work out the number in that box and what to write.

The pair carries on until they have completed the three empty boxes. For each problem, children swap roles.

At the end, the pair works together to find and shade in each set of numbers on a 100-grid, checking that the numbers in their boxes match those on the grid.

(m) *Tell me why you think 57 goes there.*

(🙂) *Do you understand what Sean is telling you to do?*

(😊) *Did you have to think carefully about what to say so that your partner could understand you?*

Support: Children refer to a 100-grid.

Extend: Children make up a grid of their own, using five squares, with one shaded, for their partner to fill in.

100-grid

As children may well need more than one grid to avoid overlapping their sets of numbers, provide write-on/wipe-off grids.

Generalising

This is a chance to draw the lesson ideas together.

Plenary

Draw eight arrows like this, with blank labels.

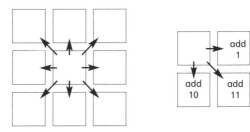

Put various numbers in the box in the centre. Work with the class to agree instructions for each arrow.

(m) *What do you think the arrow in the opposite direction will tell us to do?*

Assessment for learning

Can the children

(m) Say and write the number that is 1 or 10 more than a two-digit number? 1 or 10 less?

(🙂) Carry out their partner's instructions accurately?

(😊) Deal sensitively with any difficulties their partner experiences while working on the task?

If not

(m) Do some work modelling numbers with base-ten blocks, adding either one or ten more blocks and noting which digit changes. This will reinforce children's understanding of the different values of tens and ones.

(🙂) Ask children to repeat their partner's instructions, reminding them to ask for clarification if there is anything they do not understand.

(😊) Make sure to model sensitive behaviour yourself and show how highly you value it.

Self and peer assessment

Lesson 1: Number properties	I think	My partner thinks
(m) I can make sense of the answers I get and cross out the correct numbers.		
I can explain how I know which set of numbers to cross out.		
I help keep a record of our findings.		

Lesson 2: Ordering numbers	I think	My partner thinks
(m) I can work out which of two three-digit numbers is the higher.		
I can explain why I chose a particular place for a digit.		
I have worked well with my partner.		

Name _____

Lesson 3: Estimating quantities	I think	My partner thinks
(m) I can make a sensible estimate of a number.		
I listen carefully to what other people say.		
I feel confident about making estimates.		

Lesson 4: Adding 1 or 10	I think	My partner thinks
(m) I can write the number that is 1 or 10 more than a two-digit number. I can write the number that is 1 or 10 less than a two-digit number.		
I carry out my partner's instructions accurately.		
I think about what my partner needs me to do and say.		

Self and peer assessment

Fractions, decimals, percentages, ratio and proportion

Learning objectives

	Lessons			
	5	**6**	**7**	**8**
Maths objectives				
position halves and quarters on a number line	●			
recognise and find fractions		●		
understand that the size of the fraction depends on the size of the whole			●	
find fractions of numbers				●
Speaking and listening skills				
use precise language to explain ideas or give information	●		●	
contribute to whole-class discussion		●		
explain and justify thinking				●
Personal skills				
improve learning and performance: develop confidence in own judgements	●			
organise work: plan and manage a group task		●		●
work with others: work cooperatively with others			●	

About these lessons

Lesson 5: Fractions on a number line

Position halves and quarters on a number line

In this lesson, children put halves and quarters on a number line to help deepen their understanding of how these fractions relate to each other and to whole numbers. In the plenary, children play a game based on fractions on the number line to increase their confidence and familiarity with them.

Use precise language to explain ideas or give information

Classroom technique: One between two

Children work together to put fractions in the correct place on a number line. One child reads out a number and describes to their partner where to write the number on the line.

Improve learning and performance: develop confidence in own judgements

The structure of the number line and the pattern of numbers along it supports children as they work and helps them feel confident that they are positioning the numbers correctly.

Lesson 6: Understanding thirds

Recognise and find fractions

Children make three 'carriages' from cubes and combine these to form a 'train'. They then make fraction statements about their train, both true and false, for the other children to discuss and verify or disprove.

Contribute to whole-class discussion

Classroom technique: Devil's advocate

Statements – false or ambiguous as well as true – can be better than questions at provoking discussion. In this lesson, children present statements for the rest of the class to discuss in the plenary.

Organise work: plan and manage a group task

Children have joint responsibility for a task set by the teacher. Aiming for a clear goal supports the group as they share the management of the task.

Lesson 7: Halves, quarters and eighths

Understand that the size of the fraction depends on the size of the whole

Children work with coloured rods of various sizes and discover that which rod is described as 'half' (or 'a quarter' or 'an eighth') depends on which rod is seen as the 'whole'.

Use precise language to explain ideas or give information

Classroom technique: One between two

Children make 'fraction walls' from coloured rods, then instruct their partner how to record them on a squared grid. This is challenging work, which requires children to take great care in expressing themselves.

Work with others: work cooperatively with others

Relying on spoken language to convey meaning, rather than gesture and pointing, is demanding for children and makes a cooperative attitude all the more important.

Lesson 8: Fractions of numbers

Find fractions of numbers

Children use counters to make 'bracelets' which match simple descriptions involving fraction words. Although the basic maths is fairly simple, the activity itself is complex and challenges children to think about and justify their ideas.

Explain and justify thinking

Classroom technique: Rotating roles

Children take turns explaining to their group why they think a particular picture of a bracelet of beads represents a given fraction. For children to speak up like this, they need the confidence that their ideas will be listened to and respected. Developing this kind of climate of reasoned and tolerant debate is a vital part of a teacher's role.

Organise work: plan and manage a group task

Children start the task working in pairs, then get together in groups of six. Although the structure of the task is straightforward, the size of the group provides children with a management challenge.

Fractions on a number line

Classroom technique: One between two

Making links
In the introduction, you are making a link between the model of fractions (sharing cakes) and the number line model (numbers in order). It is important to make these links often, so that children develop a broad and flexible understanding of fractional numbers.

Telephone conversation
Alternatively, use this technique: Child A child sits at the table, with a copy of RS5 and the pencil. Child B sits with their back to the table and their own copy of RS5. Child B tells their partner where to write the number on the line. This ensures children use speech as a way of communicating.

Reading fractions
If children find it difficult to read aloud the fractional part of the number from the symbols, tell them to look underneath the line to see whether it is a half or a quarter and then above the line to see how many there are.

Introduction

Model the number $1\frac{1}{2}$ by drawing two stick people and three cakes. Discuss how to share the three cakes fairly between the two people.

one and a half cakes each
$1\frac{1}{2}$ cakes each

Establish that they each have one and a half cakes and demonstrate how to write this in words and in symbols.

Repeat this, sharing five cakes between four people to teach 'one and a quarter'.

Demonstrate how to record these fractions on the number line. Display RS5. Work with the class to put the half numbers $\frac{1}{2}$, $1\frac{1}{2}$, $2\frac{1}{2}$, $3\frac{1}{2}$, $4\frac{1}{2}$ on the 0–5 number line. As each one is placed, establish its size – for example, with $4\frac{1}{2}$, point out that it is greater than 4 and less than 5.

Read out the numbers in order with the class, emphasising the repeated pattern.

(m) *When one cake is divided in half, how many halves are there? Yes, two. And what does that two have to do with the two under the line?*

(m) *Should $4\frac{1}{2}$ go nearer the 4 or the 5? Or should it go in the middle between them? Where should $4\frac{1}{4}$ go?*

Pairs

Each pair of children works with a copy of RS5, putting the numbers in the correct places on the number line. The pair has one pencil between them. One child reads out a number from the list and tells the other child, without pointing, where to write the number.

Can you describe where to put $3\frac{1}{2}$?

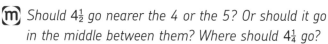

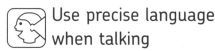
Use precise language when talking

How can you check that you understand what your partner means?

Are you feeling more certain about this work now you have done a few numbers?

Support: Children write only the halves on the number line: $\frac{1}{2}$, $1\frac{1}{2}$, $2\frac{1}{2}$, $3\frac{1}{2}$, $4\frac{1}{2}$.

Extend: Children continue the 0–5 number line to 10.

Plenary

Display a completed copy of RS5 and read through the numbers in order, emphasising the repeated pattern. Play a game with the class divided into pairs: choose a number from the line in secret and ask children to work out your number from the clues you give them.

Pairs discuss their answers and take turns to write the number on a wipe board and show it to you.

How did you know that my number was $3\frac{1}{2}$?

Pat yourselves on the back for every number you work out correctly.

Clues

For example:

I'm thinking of a number greater than 3 but less than $3\frac{1}{2}$.

I'm thinking of a number less than 2 and greater than $1\frac{1}{2}$.

I'm thinking of a number with a half in it that is greater than 4.

I'm thinking of a number that is three quarter steps less than 4.

Develop confidence in own judgements

During this lesson, you have addressed the names and order of the fractions between 0 and 5 in various ways. This approach reinforces children's basic understanding of fractions and, in turn, gives them the confidence to play this game.

Assessment for learning

Can the children

Place $2\frac{1}{2}$, $1\frac{3}{4}$ and $4\frac{1}{2}$ on the number line?

Describe to their partner where to place $2\frac{1}{2}$ or $4\frac{1}{2}$?

Say confidently why they placed a particular fraction in its position?

If not

Go back to working with half numbers such as $1\frac{1}{2}$ and $2\frac{1}{2}$. Make links with children's ages: 7, $7\frac{1}{2}$, 8, $8\frac{1}{2}$.

Ask another child to offer a description – or do so yourself – and ask the child to repeat it.

Assess children's confidence in another area of maths, but make sure they deal confidently with some of the mathematical work they are offered.

Understanding thirds
Classroom technique: Devil's advocate

Sample statements:
There are 6 blue cubes, 6 red cubes and 6 yellow cubes. (true)
There are 20 cubes altogether. (false)
One third of the cubes are red. (true)
Half of the cubes are blue. (false)

True or false
Treating correct/incorrect and true/false in a playful way can encourage children to take risks and volunteer opinions, especially if you yourself make statements that are shown to be false.

Introduction

Ask a child to choose a number between 1 and 10 (for example 6). Work with them to make three 'carriages' of that many cubes, with each carriage a different colour, and join these together to make a 'train'.

Collect in statements about the train and add some yourself, if necessary, to ensure that the idea of 'thirds' is included. Discuss each statement with the class and agree on whether it is true or false.

Write up key words from the statements and encourage children to use those later on when describing their own trains.

Key words
one third two thirds same equal half number

(m) *One third of the train is red. Are two thirds of the train yellow?*

How do you know that the carriages are the same length?

Could that statement be true? Why not?

Groups of three

Children work in groups of three. One child chooses a number between 2 and 10, and each child makes a carriage with that number of cubes, combining the carriages to form a train. As a group, they record two or more statements about their train, including at least one true and one false one.

Groups repeat this twice more so that everyone has a go at choosing the size of carriage.

(m) *Can you make a statement using the word 'half' or 'third'? Is your statement true?*

(m) *If you remove one cube from this carriage, is it still one third of the whole train?*

😊 *How can you make sure everyone in the group shares the work fairly?*

Support: Provide statements to be completed, such as: "My train has … carriages. Each carriage is … cubes long"; "My train has … cubes altogether."

Extend: Specify that there must be at least one statement containing 'third' and one containing 'two thirds'.

Plenary

Each group shows one of their trains and reads out one of their statements about that train.

> This is our train: it has 24 cubes in it altogether.
>
> Our statement is: "One third of 24 cubes is 9 cubes."

Tell your partner
This technique (p10) is useful for keeping all children involved during class sessions.

The rest of the class discuss in pairs whether the statement is true or false, indicating this with a 'thumbs up' or 'thumbs down'.

Ask groups for explanations of their thinking and encourage debate about these in the class. Use the opportunity to make statements yourself that include the key fraction words you want to give meaning to.

Thoughtful debate
It can take time to develop an atmosphere where thoughtful debate takes place. It requires both self-confidence and tolerance of others. However, it is a most valuable tool for learning in every part of the curriculum, not just mathematics.

ⓜ *Could each carriage have 9 cubes? Is 9 one third of 24?*

👤 *Are thirds always the same size? What if you added a cube to this third?*

👤 *Tell the class what you said earlier about halves and thirds.*

Assessment for learning

Can the children

ⓜ Make a true statement about their 'train', using the word 'third'?

👤 Volunteer a comment in class discussion?

😊 Work together to write statements about their train?

If not

ⓜ Do more work on dividing shapes and groups of objects into halves, quarters and thirds, focusing on the language of fractions and encouraging children to use this language.

👤 Make sure children have opportunities to do so on another occasion, prompting them by focused questions if necessary.

😊 Observe this group working again and note the dynamics that prevent children achieving their task, then rearrange the grouping so children who work efficiently can model good practice to those who work less methodically.

Halves, quarters and eighths

Classroom technique: One between two

Learning objectives

Maths
Understand that the size of the fraction depends on the size of the whole

Speaking and listening
'Use precise language when talking'
Use precise language to explain ideas or give information

Personal skills
'Work cooperatively with others'
Work with others: work cooperatively with others

Words and phrases
part, equal parts, fraction, one whole, half, halves, quarter/s, eighth/s, calculate

Resources
display set of coloured rods such as Cuisenaire for each pair:
copies of RS6
set of coloured rods (for three pairs to share)

Using fractional language
There are many ways of describing the relationship between the light and dark green rods, and it can boost children's confidence to use their own description and have it accepted by the class. This will also help them connect the fraction statements to their own statements and understand the former better.

One between two
Child A instructs Child B how to draw their wall in colour, label the rod at the base of the wall as '1' (point out that '1' means 'one whole') and label the other rods with the appropriate fraction. They then fill in some of the incomplete statements.
Children swap roles to record the next wall.

Introduction

Show the class an even-numbered rod (for example, 6) from a set of coloured rods and describe it by its colour name (for example, dark green). Ask what other rod could be doubled to make the same length as yours. Try each suggestion by putting two of them next to the dark green one and comparing the lengths. When you have established that two light greens are the same as one dark green, write up this statement:

2 light greens are equal to 1 dark green.

Children then suggest other ways of saying this. Write up each accurate suggestion, focusing on statements that use the language of fractions:

> A light green is half of a dark green.
> Light green is half, and dark green is 1.

(m) *Is one half always the same size? Could the dark green rod be one half of another rod?*

(speaking) *Tell me which rod to use next. How many do I need?*

Pairs

Children work in pairs with a copy of RS6. Child A chooses a rod to be the base of a 'wall'. Child B makes the next layer of the wall, using two equal shorter rods (this won't be possible with a base made from an odd number such as 5 or 7), and describes what they have done. Children make further layers, using four or eight rods, and describe them.

The pair builds several walls, recording each wall on RS6, using 'One between two' (p8).

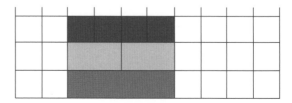

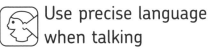
 Can you say why the white rod and the red rod both have '½' labels?

How can you tell your partner what to write without pointing?

How can you help your partner label the rods?

Support: Children draw the walls together, then fill in the statements with support from you or from a confident child as their 'peer tutor' (p8).

Extend: Children work with other fractions such as thirds or fifths.

Plenary

Use a large sheet of squared paper. With the help of the class, draw and colour a wall with a base worth 2 squares and label the layers. Repeat this with other walls, with bases worth 4, 6, 8 and 10 squares. Agree a name for each wall.

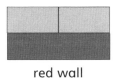   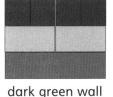

red wall   blue wall   dark green wall

Understanding fractions
This helps children focus on the idea that a fraction such as ½ or ¼ can occur in more than one wall, but that, in each case, there is the same number of them (2 halves or 4 quarters) combined to make 1.

Choose a 'brick' in secret, read out its fraction label and describe its colour. Children take turns to identify the wall it comes from.

If this blue rod was a half, how big would the whole be?

What can you tell the class about the brick you have chosen?

Assessment for learning

Can the children

Show you rods which are worth half of two different wholes?

Describe to their partner how to label the 'bricks' of the 'wall' they have drawn?

Complete one or more walls successfully, working with their partner?

If not

Do more basic work on simple fractions such as halves and quarters.

Use a 'peer tutor' (p8) to work with the pair and support the child in giving instructions to their partner.

Consider whether the pair is well suited. Emphasise that, for good cooperation, instructions given by one child need to be clear and easy to absorb by their partner and that any misunderstandings must be clarified straight away.

Fractions of numbers

Classroom technique: Rotating roles

Learning objectives

m Maths
Find fractions
of numbers

Speaking and listening
'Explain what you think
and why you think it'
Explain and justify thinking

Personal skills
'Plan and manage
a group task'
Organise work: plan and
manage a group task

W Words and phrases
half, quarter, part,
equal, whole, many, explain,
justify

r Resources
different-coloured
transparent counters
for each pair:
two slips cut from RS7
two slips cut from RS8
coloured counters
coloured pencils

Introduction

Display different-coloured transparent counters to make a 12-bead 'giant's bracelet'. Ask a volunteer to change the beads, so that half are, for example, blue. Write up statements that go with the bracelet.

12 beads
$\frac{1}{2}$ **blue**

Ask another volunteer to rearrange the beads without changing them and ask the class whether the statement still applies. Encourage debate about this, writing up some opinions, and air any misunderstandings that children have.

m *If you added another two beads, are half still blue?*

How do you know half the bracelet is blue? I've changed the order of the beads!

Encouraging debate
This kind of debate is important because it encourages children to think actively. After the debate, explain that the statement still applies, whatever the rearrangement.

Pairs/Groups of six

Give each pair of children two instruction slips from RS7. Pairs work together to model the bracelets described, using counters. They agree on the bracelets being correct and draw pictures of them, using coloured pencils, on slips cut from RS8.

Pairs then get together in groups of six, working with the six slips and six bracelet drawings. Children shuffle the slips and lay the pictures face up on the table. Each child, in turn, takes a slip and reads it out loud. They identify which picture belongs with that instruction and justify their choice to the rest of the group.

Your slip says '12 beads, $\frac{1}{2}$ green'. Could that be the picture you need? Why not?

How do you decide whose turn it is next?

Working in such a big group, what could go wrong? What must you try to avoid doing?

Dealing with confusion
There may be more than one picture which matches an instruction, or one picture may match more than one instruction. This can lead to two children identifying the same picture. If this happens and there is one picture left over, the group needs to find out which instruction it matches.

Explain and justify thinking
Justifying their choice of picture means that each child has to put their thinking into words. As this is an important part of the activity, check on each group if that is being done.

Explain what you think
and why you think it

lesson**8**

Support: Use the first three slips from RS7, which have '$\frac{1}{2}$' as
the fraction.

Extend: Use the last three slips from RS7, which have two instructions.

Plenary

Tell the class

In the plenary, there will be opportunities for explaining and rationalising. Support less confident children in taking part, using careful questions for them to answer with 'yes' or 'no' and offering them sentences to repeat.

Hold up a slip from RS7 and ask for pictures that match it. With the class, look at the pictures and check that they match the description. Allow challenges and questions and collect in suggestions of other possible pictures for the same instruction.

That could be
12 beads, $\frac{1}{4}$ yellow
or
12 beads, $\frac{1}{2}$ green
or
12 beads, $\frac{1}{12}$ blue.

Repeat with other descriptions.

(m) *How many beads are on your bracelet? Half are red. How many is that?*

(face) *Half of this 16-bead bracelet is blue, and half of that 20-bead bracelet is blue. But the numbers are 8 blue beads and 10 blue beads. Why are the numbers different?*

Assessment for learning

Can the children

(m) Say what fraction of a bracelet has, for example, red beads?

(face) Explain why their description fits the bracelet in question?

(child) Complete the group task so that everyone has a turn?

If not

(m) Focus on halves for a while, making and describing sets of cubes, counters or beads where half are, for example, red.

(face) Offer an explanation yourself and make a note to focus on the language of explanations and reasons at a later date.

(child) Help a group that has been successful at managing the task to talk to the class about what they did to achieve this.

Self and peer assessment

Lesson 5: Fractions on a number line	I think	My partner thinks
(m) I can put these fractions on a number line: _____		
(peer) I can tell my partner where to put a fraction on the number line.		
(self) I can say whether or not I feel sure about where I have put a fraction.		

Lesson 6: Understanding thirds	I think	My partner thinks
(m) I can say something about our 'train', using the word 'third'.		
(peer) I talk about my ideas in a group.		
(self) I help my group do the work we have been set.		

Name _____

Lesson 7: Halves, quarters and eighths	I think	My partner thinks
(m) I can find a rod and another rod which is worth half of it.		
(👤) I can tell my partner how to label the 'bricks' on the 'wall' they have drawn.		
(☺) I work with my partner to finish the task we have been set.		

Lesson 8: Fractions of numbers	I think	My partner thinks
(m) I can make a bracelet with $\frac{1}{2}$ or $\frac{1}{4}$ of the beads the same colour.		
(👤) I can make a fraction statement about my bracelet and say why it is true.		
(☺) I help my group make sure that everyone has a turn.		

Self and peer assessment

Addition and subtraction

Learning objectives

	Lessons			
	9	**10**	**11**	**12**
Maths objectives				
develop mental calculation strategies	●			
use an empty number line to add and subtract		●		
know by heart addition and subtraction facts to 10			●	
add a single digit to a two-digit number				●
Speaking and listening skills				
listen with sustained concentration	●			
share and discuss ideas and reach consensus		●		
reach a common understanding with a partner			●	
contribute to small-group discussion				●
Personal skills				
organise work: plan ways to solve a problem	●			
work with others: overcome difficulties and recover from mistakes		●		
improve learning and performance: assess learning progress			●	
improve learning and performance: reflect on learning				●

About these lessons

Lesson 9: Analysing addition methods

(m) Develop mental calculation strategies

Children add together sets of four numbers, then explain how they did so to another child. This is a challenging activity, but it presents an opportunity for children to put into practice some of the mental strategies they have learned as well as to learn about new ones.

Listen with sustained concentration

Classroom technique: Rotating roles

In one role, children have to put their thinking into words. In another role, they must ask questions and listen to the answers. This second role is given importance because children may be called on in the plenary to explain what they found out in their role as 'listener'.

Organise work: plan ways to solve a problem

Children are faced with several numbers to add, but are left to choose their own strategies for starting, continuing, completing and checking the addition.

Lesson 10: Mental calculation strategies

(m) Use an empty number line to add and subtract

There are many ways of doing addition and subtraction calculations on an empty number line. In this activity, children discuss how to do such problems, supported by their partner and group.

Share and discuss ideas and reach consensus

Classroom technique: Peer tutoring

Children work in mixed-ability pairs, with the more confident child who acts as 'tutor' making sure that their 'pupil' share their understanding of the task. The sharing and discussing of ideas – in this activity, understanding a number line technique – gives focus to children's talk.

Work with others: overcome difficulties and recover from mistakes

Children who find the work too hard need encouragement and support not only from the teacher but also from their peers. Pairing them with a more able child gives them the opportunity to learn from that child how to tackle the problem.

Lesson 11: Practising number bonds

(m) Know by heart addition and subtraction facts to 10

This game involves mental addition in several ways: first, children must find numbers that add up to 10 or less, then add several small numbers and, finally, add four two-digit numbers. In all of these additions, a thorough knowledge of addition and subtraction facts to 10 is a great benefit.

Reach a common understanding with a partner

Classroom technique: Talking partners

Children play in teams of two. Teams must discuss how to best use the dice numbers they roll and share the work of adding their scores.

Improve learning and performance: assess learning progress

In the plenary, children look at the list of mental strategies produced by the class to assess which ones they used during the game and which ones they could try next time they play.

Lesson 12: Addition with two-digit numbers

(m) Add a single digit to a two-digit number

Children play a game where they add a single digit to a two-digit number. This requires a knowledge of number bonds to 10 and an understanding of place value in order to choose the best card to play.

Contribute to small-group discussion

Classroom technique: Heads or tails/1, 2, 3, 4

Children discuss their strategies, first with their partner, then in the whole group. They know that, in the plenary, the technique '1, 2, 3, 4', adjusted to six children here, will decide which member of the group speaks, so all are encouraged to take responsibility for joining in the group discussion.

Improve learning and performance: reflect on learning

In the plenary, children discuss what maths they have been learning or practising in playing the game.

Analysing addition methods
Classroom technique: Rotating roles

Learning objectives

m Maths
Develop mental calculation strategies

Speaking and listening
'Listen well'
Listen with sustained concentration

Personal skills
'Plan ways to solve a problem'
Organise work: plan ways to solve a problem

W Words and phrases
addition, more, plus, make, sum, total, altogether, check, calculate, method, jotting

r Resources
for each group:
cards A, B and C cut from RS9
pencils and paper

Introduction

Write up four numbers between 0 and 50 to be added together. Ask for three suggestions about how to start and scribe these:

---

5   24   7   16

Add the two small numbers.

Start with the biggest.

Add the 24 and the 5.

Encourage the class to help you work out the final answer for each suggestion.

---

5   24   7   16

Ruari's suggestion:

Add 5 and 7 in your head to get 12:   12   24   16

Add all the tens: 10 + 20 + 10 = 40

Add all the ones: 2 + 4 + 6 = 12

Add the tens and the ones: 40 + 10 + 2 = 52

Jottings
Explain how to use jottings to keep track of where you are in the calculation, so that children have a good model to follow when they work independently.

Remind children to check their work.

m *How would you add 24 and 16?*

m *Jess got a different answer to Ruari. Let's check which calculation has gone wrong.*

(S) *Can you tell me in your own words what Ruari suggested we do next?*

Groups of three

Making connections
This activity combines mental calculation strategies and pencil-and-paper methods. As children talk through what they did, a process of integration takes place, linking both methods in their minds.

Children work in groups of three with cards A, B and C cut from RS9. Each child takes a different card and adds the numbers, recording on paper how they did it. The group swap the cards so that each child completes a second addition. For each card there will be one child who has not added the numbers: this child acts as 'teacher' and asks the other two to explain their methods. The group repeat this for the other cards so that everyone has a turn at being 'teacher'.

The group then choose a 'teacher' for the plenary. That child must ensure they know the four numbers added and what methods their 'pupils' used.

(m) *When you added those numbers, what did you do first? What did you do next? Why did you do that?*

(👂) *Do you understand what your 'pupil' said? Do you need to make notes?*

(🙂) *Look at those numbers and read them out. Can you see two that you could add easily?*

Support: Use cards with single-digit numbers from the top row of RS9.

Extend: Use cards with larger numbers from the bottom row of RS9. Alternatively, children invent their own set of four numbers to add.

Listening skills

This part of the lesson has similarities with 'Ticket to explain' (p11), where a child must re-explain the previous child's method before outlining their own. Here, however, the child is only explaining other children's methods.

Involving children

Children who themselves added the numbers in question give you a 'thumbs up' if they used the method described and a 'thumbs down' if they used a different method.

Plenary

The groups' chosen 'teachers' explain what their 'pupils' did with one set of numbers.

Scribe the methods as in the introduction and help children draw out common themes such as: adding numbers to get a multiple of ten; doubling or near doubling; adding a near multiple of ten or adjusting.

(m) *Why is adding on 11 easy? What do you do?*

(🙂) *Why is it a good idea to start by adding the 9 and the 11?*

Assessment for learning

Can the children

(m) Use mental calculation strategies they have been taught to add the numbers they are given?

(👂) Listen to what their 'pupil' says and repeat back all or some of it?

(🙂) Choose where to start when adding four numbers?

If not

(m) Do more work on describing, naming and sharing children's own strategies.

(👂) Offer work on listening to ideas and explanations given to the class by you or another child and repeating them to a partner.

(🙂) Spend five minutes at the beginning of lessons looking at sets of numbers and discussing in pairs how to add them, without actually doing the addition.

Mental calculation strategies
Classroom technique: Peer tutoring

Learning objectives

 Maths
Use an empty number line to add and subtract

Speaking and listening
'Share ideas and reach agreement'
Share and discuss ideas and reach consensus

Personal skills
'Get over difficulties and mistakes'
Work with others: overcome difficulties and recover from mistakes

Words and phrases
add, addition, total, double, subtract, subtraction, difference, minus, equals, answer, method, solution, check

Resources
for each pair:
two copies of RS10
0–6 or 0–9 dice

Working mentally
If children prefer to work mentally, acknowledge this and ask them to use the empty number line to demonstrate their mental processes.

Using the dice numbers
For example,
dice numbers: 4 3 1 6
Arranging them as follows

| 4 | 6 | + | 1 | 3 |

gives an easy calculation.

Peer tutoring
Observe children at work and identify those who are confident and accurate with the empty number line. Give these children the title of 'Number Line Expert' and ask them to work with individuals needing support. This may mean rearranging some pairs halfway through the lesson.

Introduction

Work with the class on using an empty number line for doing addition and subtraction calculations. Present a calculation. Children discuss in pairs how they would do this on an empty number line.

Emphasise that there is often more than one way to reach a solution.

$$22 + 43$$
$$\text{turn it around} \to 43 + 22$$

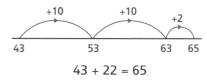

$$43 + 22 = 65$$

Read out the number sentence with your partner and talk about what it means.

Pairs

Children work in mixed-ability pairs, with a copy of RS10 each. For each question, children roll the dice as many times as there are empty boxes and write the digits on the sheet. They then discuss how to put the digits in the boxes to form a calculation that makes sense.

Pairs discuss how to do the calculation, mentally or using an empty number line, do it and write the answer in the oval on RS10.

Pairs check the answer in one of two ways. If they found it mentally, they check by using an empty number line. If they used the line first time, they use it again, but with a different method, to help them identify and correct any errors.

Pairs continue in the same way with the other questions.

m What numbers will you put on your number line? Tell me about the jumps you are going to do.

m With that calculation, what do you need to find out?

Tell your partner how you would work out that answer.

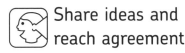
 *How are you both working on that problem?*

Support: Use peer tutors to model and teach empty number line methods.

Extend: Children choose the digits themselves, aiming to form calculations that will challenge them.

Plenary

Pairs get together in groups of four and talk about their experience of working in this way.

Children think in private about what they have learned from the experience.

Experts, do you think you have learned anything from being a tutor?

Those of you who were helped by a tutor, do you think you understand more now about using an empty number line?

Topics for discussion
– what was it like writing their own calculations
– what was it like being a Number Line Expert
– what was it like being tutored by a Number Line Expert
– how confident they feel about using the empty number line

Number Line Experts
The title of 'Expert' can be carried over into other lessons, though it is important not to overdo the amount of tutoring children do. Try to identify other children as other kinds of Expert, so that the sense of achievement it gives is shared as widely as possible.

Assessment for learning

Can the children

Ⓜ Use an empty number line to carry out or check a calculation?

Tell their partner how they would use an empty number line to do a calculation?

Accept the support of a peer tutor?

If not

Ⓜ Ask children to talk you through some calculations they can do mentally and model these on an empty number line while they watch. This helps children see how the line models and supports mental strategies.

See if children can actually draw and use the number line. As they do so, put into words for them what they are doing.

Find out who they would like to help them and try using this person as a tutor. Consider using the child as an 'Expert' in some other area (perhaps not mathematics) to help them warm to the idea.

Practising number bonds
Classroom technique: Talking partners

Learning objectives

m Maths
Know by heart addition and subtraction facts to 10

Speaking and listening
'Reach an understanding with your partner'
Reach a common understanding with a partner

Personal skills
'Assess your progress in learning'
Improve learning and performance: assess learning progress

W Words and phrases
addition, sum, total, altogether, method, mental strategy, check

r Resources
for each group:
two 1–9 dice
two sets of
1–12 number cards

Introduction

Demonstrate a game by playing against the class. Lay out two sets of number cards, face up, one for each team (you and the class). Roll two 1–9 dice and find the total. Turn over one or more of your cards to the same total value – for example, roll 4 and 5 and turn over 9, or 8 and 1, or 6, 2 and 1.

Dice numbers: 4 and 5

9 already turned over

Turn over 7 and 2.

Roll two dice for the class and invite suggestions for cards to turn over for their team.

When one team cannot turn over any cards, finish that round, then stop playing. Each team now scores the total value of their cards left face up. Play two games and total the scores for the two games to find the overall winner: whoever has the lower score wins.

m *What numbers there could make 13? And what else?*

Speaking *Talk with your partner about which numbers your team should turn over.*

Reach a common understanding with a partner
When a game is over, pairs discuss strategies for adding the numbers still showing.

Discussion
It is important that team members check each other's arithmetic and talk about the possibilities with each throw. Encourage children to look hard at what cards to turn over as the obvious is not always the most suitable.

Adding numbers
Encourage children to find ways of sharing the work of adding their scores. One child could add and the other check the total, or they could work together, checking each other's calculations as they go along.

Groups of four

Children play the game in teams of two. Child A from the first team rolls the dice and finds the total, both children discuss possible cards to turn over and reach a decision, and Child B turns the cards over.

Children play four games and total the scores to find the overall winner – the team with the lower score.

m *If 1 and 8 makes 9, then 2 and ... what number also makes 9?*

Speaking *Sam says you might not get another chance to turn over 7. Why do you think that is?*

Support: Use 1–6 dice. Provide a number line for children to model their additions on.

Extend: Use 1–20 number cards and three dice.

Plenary

Display three or more of the number cards used in the game. Children discuss in pairs how they would add the numbers. Collect in suggestions for strategies and scribe these:

> **1 2 3 8 10**
>
> Add 2 and 8 because they make 10.
>
> Add 10 and 8 because they are
> the big numbers.

Repeat with other sets of numbers and explain general strategies.

> **Strategies for adding several numbers**
> Look for numbers that make 10.
> Start with the big numbers.
> Add 9 by adding 10 and taking off 1.

Playing again
Keep the list of general strategies and revise them when children next play the game.

Finally, ask children to look at the list of strategies and discuss with their partner which ones they used during the game and which ones they could try next time they play.

(m) *Which of these numbers add up to 10?*

Do you think you and your partner would try this method for adding 9? Talk about it together.

Did you try any new strategies today?

Assessment for learning

Can the children

(m) Use addition and subtraction facts to 10 when choosing which number cards to turn over?

Discuss and agree with a partner what choices to make in the game?

Decide on what strategies they could try to use next time they play?

If not

(m) Give pairs of children responsibility for finding out some number bonds their partner doesn't know.

Make sure children take turns at decision making and always explain their reasons to their partner.

Set some calculations where a particular strategy would work well. Ask a confident child to describe how they would use that strategy, then ask everybody to use it to solve each calculation.

Addition with two-digit numbers

Classroom technique: Heads or tails/1, 2, 3, 4

Learning objectives

(m) Maths
Add a single digit to a two-digit number

Speaking and listening
'Join in a discussion with a small group'
Contribute to small-group discussion

Personal skills
'Think about what you have learned'
Improve learning and performance: reflect on learning

(w) Words and phrases
addition, sum, total, multiple, method, strategy, two-digit number, check

(r) Resources
for each group:
two sets of
0–10 number cards
calculator
counters

Teamwork
If one child holds the cards, their partner presses the buttons on the calculator. In the next game, they swap. Each pair discusses the possibilities before playing a card: only when both players agree should the card be played.

A final check
When the last card is played, the total should be 110. This means the last player automatically gets a counter.

Why three teams?
With only two players/teams, one player is often caught on the defensive and has to keep adding to a multiple of 10, thus allowing the other player to make a multiple of 10 again. With three players, this is avoided.

The end of a game
If the final total is not 110, something has gone wrong somewhere. All six players will need to agree whether to replay the game or carry on.

Introduction

Use the 'Goldfish bowl' technique (p13) to demonstrate a game. Shuffle two sets of number cards, share out the cards between three players and turn the last card face up. Display the value of that card on a calculator. The first player looks at their cards and chooses one to put face up on top of that card. They add the value of their card to the value of the starting card, using the calculator. If the total is 10 or a multiple of 10, that player takes a counter from a central pile.

> If we use the 3, we can make 20 and win a counter.

Play continues like this, adding to the running total (don't clear the display after each turn). Each time a player makes a multiple of 10, they take a counter.

(m) *What is a good way of adding 9 to a number?*

(m) *Which number would you choose to put down next? Why?*

Groups of six

Children play the game in teams of two, with three teams in a game.

They play three or six games consecutively so that each team gets an equal opportunity to start and finish.

Towards the end of the session, children reflect a few minutes on their own on how they chose what card to play each time, any mistakes they made and how they could avoid these next time, then discuss with their partner and, finally, with the whole group.

(m) *What does 7 and 3 make? So 27 and 3 makes …?*

(speaking) *Why is zero a useful number to have?*

(speaking) *Tell your group how you worked out that 42 and 8 makes 50.*

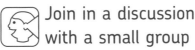
Support: Children play the game in pairs of two with one set of number cards. The final total will be 55.

Extend: Groups play with all three hands laid face up on the table so that everybody can see the cards. This is quite a complicated game in which players try to avoid giving the next player the chance. Don't reset the calculator to zero after each game: it should show 660 after six games.

Plenary

Strategy
Some players will work out that they can save a 10 or 0 until a multiple of 10 is reached by the previous player and then play it, ensuring a counter.

Two or more groups tell the class about the strategies they discovered and the mistakes they made. Using '1, 2, 3, 4' (p12; adjusted to six children) number the children and roll a dice to decide who will report back.

Briefly discuss what maths children have been learning or practising in playing the game, focusing on strategies for adding single digits to a two-digit number.

(m) *If the total so far is 66, what would be a good number to play?*

(☺) *What numbers do you find easy to add on, without using your fingers? What numbers are harder?*

Assessment for learning

Can the children

(m) Find an appropriate way to add a single digit to a two-digit number?

(☺) Join in the discussion with their group?

(☺) Name one or more things they have been learning or practising in the lesson?

If not

(m) Use 'Peer tutoring' (p8) so that children can teach each other useful ways of adding single digits to a two-digit number.

(☺) Introduce a 'talking stick' (p10) to give children turns at speaking in a group.

(☺) Make a point of specifying to children what they are learning in each lesson, or part of a lesson, so that they get used to thinking in these terms.

Self and peer assessment

Lesson 9: Analysing addition methods	I think	My partner thinks
(m) I can add several numbers.		
I listen to the other people in my group.		
I can choose which numbers to start with if I have several numbers to add.		

Lesson 10: Mental calculation strategies	I think	My partner thinks
(m) I can use an empty number line to do a calculation.		
I can tell my partner how to do a calculation on an empty number line.		
I help my partner and let them help me.		

Name _____

Lesson 11: Practising number bonds	I think	My partner thinks
(m) I can add several small numbers quickly.		
(face) I talk with my partner about what cards to turn over.		
(face) I am learning to use different methods for adding numbers.		

Lesson 12: Addition with two-digit numbers	I think	My partner thinks
(m) I can add any single digit to a two-digit number.		
(face) I join in the talking with my group when we are asked to discuss something.		
(face) One thing I have been learning or practising in this lesson is: _____		

Self and peer assessment

Multiplication and division

Learning objectives

	Lessons			
	13	**14**	**15**	**16**
Maths objectives				
derive doubles of numbers	●			
derive halves of numbers		●		
know by heart multiplication facts in the 2, 5 and 10 times tables			●	
understand division as grouping or sharing				●
Speaking and listening skills				
explain and justify thinking	●			●
reach a common understanding with a partner		●		
contribute to small-group discussion			●	
Personal skills				
work with others: give feedback sensitively	●			
improve learning and performance: take pride in work		●		
organise work: use different approaches to tackle a problem			●	
work with others: work cooperatively with others				●

About these lessons

Lesson 13: Doubling two-digit numbers

(m) Derive doubles of numbers

In this lesson, children practise doubling two-digit numbers. They work mainly with numbers where the ones digit is 5 or less, thus keeping the calculations simple. Extension questions lead them into more challenging territory.

Explain and justify thinking

Classroom technique: One between two

Children work in pairs to double numbers. One child takes the role of 'Solver' and explains to their partner how to double a number. The other child, the 'Recorder', keeps a written record and challenges anything they disagree with.

Work with others: give feedback sensitively

In the plenary, children turn to their partner and say one thing they have enjoyed about working together on the task. Telling children in advance that this will happen encourages them to think about how they themselves are to work with during the lesson.

Lesson 14: Halving numbers

(m) Derive halves of numbers

Children work on doubling the same numbers as in the previous lesson, then present their doubles to other children who must find the original numbers by undoing the doubling – in effect, halving them. This activity helps clarify the link between doubling and halving, which children sometimes find problematic.

Reach a common understanding with a partner

Classroom technique: Peer tutoring

If a child has difficulties halving a number, the child who doubled the original number acts as peer tutor and explains how they doubled it, helping their partner reverse the steps to halve the number.

Improve learning and performance: take pride in work

Children are encouraged to take pride not only in their ability to halve numbers but also in their achievement in helping their partner.

Lesson 15: Multiplication problem solving

(m) Know by heart multiplication facts in the 2, 5 and 10 times tables

Children try to achieve a target by multiplying digits by 2, 5 and 10 and adding the results. While the main focus is on solving the problem, children rehearse many multiplication facts in working towards a solution.

Contribute to small-group discussion

Classroom technique: Talking partners

Children work with a partner, aiming to make three different targets, then compare their results with two other pairs who worked with the same numbers. Working first with just one partner helps children develop the confidence to contribute to discussion in the group of six.

Organise work: use different approaches to tackle a problem

Children are restricted by having only 12 number cards to use in reaching three targets. They are unlikely to solve the problem first time, and will have to try different tactics as they juggle the various possibilities.

Lesson 16: Practising division

(m) Begin to find remainders after division

Children generally find division the hardest of the four arithmetical operations. They may struggle particularly with the two different models of sharing and grouping. The kind of practical activity described in this lesson is useful in clarifying these two different aspects.

Explain and justify thinking

Classroom technique: One between two

One child is the 'Calculator' and the other the 'Recorder'. The Calculator moves the counters according to their chosen method, explaining to their partner what they are doing and responding to any questions or challenges posed by their partner.

Work with others: work cooperatively with others

Sharing a task means children must cooperate in order to achieve their aim.

Doubling two-digit numbers
Classroom technique: One between two

Learning objectives

(m) Maths
Derive doubles
of numbers

Speaking and listening
'Explain what you think
and why you think it'
Explain and justify thinking

Personal skills
'Give feedback sensitively'
Work with others: give feedback
sensitively

(W) Words and phrases
double, halve, half,
add, multiply, tens, ones,
digit, solve, record, answer

(r) Resources
cubes or base-ten
blocks (optional)
for each pair:
copy of RS11
1–6 dice
pencil

Modelling
Modelling the numbers with
base-ten blocks can help children
develop the mental imagery
which will support them in
doubling numbers independently.

Tell your partner
Pause after choosing each
number and ask children to
agree with their partner how to
double it before inviting one pair
to offer a solution.

One between two
The 'Solver's' job is to put their
thinking into words so that the
'Recorder' knows what to write
down. Accept long-winded and
repetitive workings-out at this
stage; more condensed versions
will come naturally once
children's understanding
is secure.

Introduction

Display a number such as 14, using base-ten blocks
or sticks of cubes, and establish the number.

Silently double the number by putting out more
base-ten blocks or cubes. Children talk to their
neighbour about what you have done.

Collect in suggestions and discuss these. Establish that
there are two ways of describing what you have done:
as an addition (for example, "I've added another 14")
and as a multiplication (for example, "I've made two
lots of 14").

Display the number grid on RS11. Choose a number
and demonstrate how to work out its double by
doubling the tens and the ones separately.

(m) *We have talked about how to double 14. How could
you double 24?*

(📢) *Why is it not good enough just to double the 4?
Why do you need to double the 10, too?*

Pairs

Children work in pairs with a copy of RS11. Child A
takes the role of 'Solver' and explains how to double a
number. Child B acts as the 'Recorder'. They throw the
dice twice to count along and down the grid to find the
number to double and circle it. Child A doubles the
number, and Child B records the answer on a piece of
paper. Children swap roles for each new number.

(m) *85 is more than 50, so its double must be more
than 100. Does that make sense?*

(m) *If you split the 45 into tens and ones, what would
you get?*

(📢) *You are right that double 300 is 600. Can you
explain how you know?*

Support: Children choose numbers from RS11 they feel confident working with. Once they have doubled several, they look back over the numbers and try some they rejected as 'too hard'.

Extend: Children add a digit to each of the numbers on RS11 and double the new numbers.

Plenary

Display RS11. Pairs choose a number they could double easily and tell the class how they did it.

Children turn to their partner and tell them one thing they have enjoyed about working together in this lesson.

m *This pair is doubling 16. See if they did it the same way you did.*

m *To double 150, this pair doubled 100, that's 200. And they doubled 50, that's 100: 200 and 100 is 300. Could you use that method to double 250?*

Tell us why you doubled your number that way.

Think for a minute about your partner's feedback and see if there is something you would like them to say next time.

Assessment for learning

Can the children

m Double these numbers: 20, 16, 32, 150, 170?

Explain how they double a number?

Tell their partner one thing they have enjoyed about working together?

If not

m Do some more practical work on doubling numbers less than 10 and explain what doubling involves: making the same number again and adding the two.

Partner the child with a confident child who will model the kind of explanation required when it is their turn to be the 'Solver'.

Ask children to reflect on their own skills at working together, out loud or on paper, and ask their partner if they agree.

Halving numbers

Classroom technique: Peer tutoring

Learning objectives

Learning objectives

m Maths
Derive halves
of numbers

Speaking and listening
'Reach an understanding
with your partner'
Reach a common
understanding with a partner

Personal skills
'Take pride in your work'
Improve learning and
performance: take pride in work

W Words and phrases
digit, two-digit
number, double, halve,
multiply, odd, even, divide,
explain, check

r Resources
cubes or base-ten
blocks (optional)
for each pair:
two copies of RS11

Introduction

Secretly write down a two-digit number less than 50, with the ones digit 4 or less. Double it and write up the answer. Explain what you have done and encourage children to discuss with their neighbour how to find your original number.

> 64
>
> What number did I double?

Establish that to undo your doubling, the number must be halved. Use cubes or base-ten blocks to show your double and, with the class, halve each part and agree your original number.

Repeat this halving with a multiple of 10.

> 50 cannot be split into
> two identical lots of 10.
> So cut one ten in half, then halve
> the remaining tens → 5 and 20 → 25

Demonstrate halving an even number with the ones digit 6 or more.

> With 36, the tens cannot be split
> into two identical lots of 10.
> So cut one ten in half, then halve
> the remaining tens and ones
> → 5 and 10 and 3 → 18

Invite a child to whisper to you a number less than 50, then to tell the class what its double is. Pairs work together to find the original number. Collect in suggestions from the class.

m *Does it matter which part of the number you halve first?*

You can be proud of yourselves for halving that number – it was quite difficult.

Halving and doubling

Doubling a number, then halving it to get back to the original, helps children link doubling and halving and begin to understand them as inverse operations.

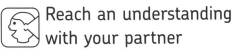

Reach an understanding with your partner

Peer tutors
The child who doubled the number has their copy of RS11 with 10 circled numbers as a prompt. They may want to check their partner's work, matching their answers against this sheet.

Prepare for the plenary
Note which children offer clear explanations so you can invite them to speak in the plenary.

Take pride in work
Tell children that the purpose of the lesson was not just about halving numbers but about learning how to help others. Encourage children to acknowledge their achievements in this, both to each other and to themselves.

Pairs

Children choose ten numbers on RS11, circle them, work out the doubles and write these underneath. They then write out the doubles again on a separate sheet of paper. Children swap their sheet of doubles with their partner who must find the originals by halving each number. If there are any numbers they have difficulty halving, they circle them for the moment.

Pairs look at the problematic halvings. The child who doubled the original number now acts as peer tutor and explains how they doubled it, working with the other child to reverse the steps to halve the number.

(m) *Does splitting that number into tens and ones help you?*

(☺) *Do you understand everything your partner is saying?*

Support: Arrange pairs of similar ability, encouraging all children to act as peer tutors, whatever their ability level.

Extend: Children choose 'harder' numbers or think up their own.

Plenary

A few children show the class how they halved a number from their sheet. Finally, have a class discussion on the experience of acting as peer tutor.

(m) *Did anyone else find half of 190? How did you do it?*

(☺) *Pat yourself on the back if you tried to help your partner with the halvings they found difficult.*

Assessment for learning

Can the children

(m) Find half of these numbers: 60, 24, 30, 600, 140?

(☺) Repeat what their partner, acting as peer tutor, has just explained to them?

(☺) Identify something about their work in the lesson that they feel proud of?

If not

(m) Do the same exercise as in the lesson, but let the child find half of the numbers they themselves have doubled.

(☺) Have a classroom blitz on listening to each other and repeating what was said.

(☺) Ask the child's partner to identify what they think the child did well.

Multiplication problem solving
Classroom technique: Talking partners

Learning objectives

m **Maths**
Know by heart multiplication facts in the 2, 5 and 10 times tables

Speaking and listening
'Join in a discussion with a small group'
Contribute to small-group discussion

Personal skills
'Try different ways to tackle a problem'
Organise work: use different approaches to tackle a problem

w **Words and phrases**
multiply, times, groups of, lots of, add, total, problem, solve, check

r **Resources**
display copy
of RS12
0–100 number line
for each group:
six or more copies
of RS12
0–9 dice
0–6 dice (optional)
three sets of
digit cards (1–9
and three 0s)

Zero
Multiplying by zero rather than leaving out a number may seem tedious. However, it can help develop an understanding of the idea that if a number is multiplied by zero, the result is zero.

Try different ways to tackle a problem
Restricting the number of cards means children will have to try various arrangements, and may find no 'perfect' solutions. This entails discussion and (polite) argument, as children choose between two places where they want to use a number.

Prepare for the plenary
Note any pairs who achieve 'difficult' targets or use interesting methods and ask them to record their solutions, to discuss later in the plenary.

Introduction

Choose a target number between 20 and 100 (for example, 53). Display one column from RS12 and collect in suggestions for numbers between 0 and 9 to put in the three empty spaces to give a total of 53 or as close as possible.

Scribe the suggestions and discuss them with the class.

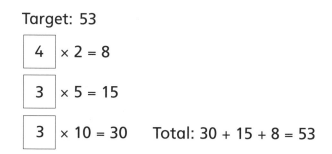

Target: 53

4	× 2 = 8
3	× 5 = 15
3	× 10 = 30 Total: 30 + 15 + 8 = 53

Use a 0–100 number line to model the jumps of 10, 5 and 1 or sketch an empty number line.

m *How many tens do we need to get close to 53?*

**Talk with the others in your group about what numbers we could try.*

**Is that the best we can do? Is there another way to get to 53?*

Groups of six

Children work in groups of six as three teams of two, each with a copy of RS12. Each team rolls a 0–9 dice twice to make a two-digit number and records this. The three numbers form the targets for all three teams, which they write on their sheets.

Each team has a set of 1–9 digit cards and three 0 cards. Their aim is to get as close to all three targets as possible.

Having completed the targets, all three teams compare their solutions. There is no winner, but teams should note how many targets they hit before repeating the activity.

m *Tell me why you are putting the 4 there.*

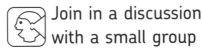 Join in a discussion with a small group

Explain to your group what you do first when you are trying to make a target.

Did anyone in your group manage to make that target? Could you make that target the same way?

Support: Children use 1–6 dice to make target numbers.

Extend: Introduce a points system: 5 points for a target made exactly; 2 points for a target plus or minus 1; 1 point for a target plus or minus 4.

Plenary

Invite one of the pairs you identified earlier to write up their 'interesting' target and give the rest of the class a minute or two to discuss in pairs how they could make this target with their digit cards. The pair in question then explains how they achieved the target (perhaps using the number line to show the jumps involved).

Why was it helpful today to know your 2, 5 and 10 times tables?

This pair's target was 77. They used 6 tens, 3 fives and 1 two. Could you make 77 a different way?

Heads or tails
Tell pairs beforehand that you will use this technique (p12) to decide which partner speaks to the class, so that both can prepare their presentation.

Assessment for learning

Can the children

Use multiplication facts accurately when working on the problems?

Take a turn at speaking when joining in the group discussion?

Recognise when one way of using the digit cards is not working and try a different arrangement?

If not

Provide a multiplication chart and encourage children to continue with the work: using the facts in solving the problem is one way of learning them.

Use a 'talking stick' (p10) to formalise the roles of 'Speaker' and 'Listeners'. Make sure Listeners are taking in what is said by occasionally asking them to repeat what another child has said.

Have a mini-plenary halfway through the lesson and ask groups to get together to discuss how they are getting on. Consider changing pairs round so children work with a partner they can learn useful tactics from.

Practising division

Classroom technique: One between twos

Learning objectives

m **Maths**
Begin to find remainders after division

Speaking and listening
'Explain what you think and why you think it'
Explain and justify thinking

Personal skills
'Work cooperatively with others'
Work with others: work cooperatively with others

W **Words and phrases**
divide, division, dividing, grouping, sharing, fair, same number, equal groups

r **Resources**
counters
whiteboard
display copy of RS14
for each pair:
copy of RS13
1–6 dice
20 counters

An image for sharing
Tell children to think of sharing as dividing out sweets fairly between a number of children – what you don't know is how many sweets each will get.

An image for grouping
Tell children to think of grouping as putting fancy fruits into packages, so each package has the correct number of fruits – what you don't know is how many packages you can fill.

Remainders
In the course of this work, children will have to deal with remainders, which is an important aspect of division. If remainders are always avoided in the interests of simplicity, children may get a distorted view of what division is all about.

Working cooperatively
Children will need to agree who takes on these responsibilities.

Running commentary
Encourage children to give a running commentary, because this will help to establish and clarify the principles of what is going on.

Introduction

Explain that you are going to demonstrate two practical methods of division: sharing and grouping and remainders.

Ask for a number between 20 and 30 (for example, 25) and show that number of counters on a whiteboard. Ask for another number between 2 and 6 (for example, 3). Divide 25 counters by 3, using sharing, and write the equation to go with it:

> 1 each ... 2 each ... 3 each ...
>
> 8 each and 1 left over
>
> 25 ÷ 3 = 8 remainder 1

Start again with the same two numbers and divide the counters, using grouping.

> Take a group of 3 counters away from the 25, and another 3, and another 3 ...
>
> I've got 8 groups and 1 left over.
>
> 25 ÷ 3 = 8 remainder 1

Pairs of children model the two methods of division with two new numbers.

m *Imagine you are putting 23 eggs into egg boxes, six in this one, six in that ... How many boxes can you fill?*

Why do you think there won't be any left over?

Pairs

Working with 1–6 dice, 20 counters and a copy of RS13, pairs of children choose a number from 10 to 20 and roll the dice to find what number to divide it by. (If they get a 1, they roll the dice again.)

Child A is the 'Calculator' and Child B the 'Recorder'. The Calculator chooses whether to use sharing or grouping and counts out the correct number of counters. They then move the counters according to the chosen method, explaining to their partner what they are doing and instructing them what to record.

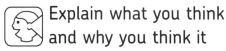 Explain what you think and why you think it

The pair carries out the other method of doing the same division before swapping roles.

(m) *Which are you doing now: grouping or sharing? How do you remember which is which?*

Support: Use sharing on this occasion.

Extend: Children predict the result before using the counters.

Plenary

Display RS14 and fill it in with results from the children's work. As the results build up, encourage children to look for any patterns.

Start a group discussion of the patterns in each column: for example:

> • As you go down the rows, the remainders increase by 1.
>
> • The remainders get to one less than the number you are dividing by, then they revert to zero.

Children use the patterns to predict any missing results, adding these to the table.

(☺) *What has your group said about the patterns on this chart?*

(☺) *What belongs in this part of the chart? How do you know?*

(☺) *What is important to do when you are discussing this in a group?*

Four numbers

There are four numbers involved in these divisions: the original number of counters, the number of piles, the number of counters in each pile and the number of counters left over. Children become easily confused between these, but the combination of a practical situation and the opportunity to talk about it with a partner usually ensures clarity.

Assessment for learning

Can the children

(m) Carry out a division accurately, using counters, both as a grouping and a sharing?

(☺) Give a running commentary on what they are doing?

(☺) Complete several divisions successfully, working with their partner?

If not

(m) Focus on sharing and grouping separately. Relate both kinds of division to real-world problem solving such as sharing out digit cards or pencils and putting paint pots or eggs into containers (grouping).

(☺) Model this yourself when carrying out calculations and encourage children to use the same technique to keep track of what they are doing.

(☺) Talk about what 'working cooperatively' means and write up some cooperative working aims to refer to in future lessons.

Self and peer assessment

Lesson 13: Doubling two-digit numbers	I think	My partner thinks
(m) I can double these numbers: _____		
I can explain how I double a number.		
I can tell my partner one thing I enjoyed about working together.		

Lesson 14: Halving numbers	I think	My partner thinks
(m) I can find half of these numbers: _____		
I listen to my partner and try to understand what they are saying.		
I can say something I did in this lesson that I feel proud of.		

Name _____

Lesson 15: Multiplication problem solving	I think	My partner thinks
(m) I can multiply numbers by 2, 5 or 10.		
I take a turn at speaking in a group discussion.		
I try another way to solve a problem if something we tried doesn't work.		

Lesson 16: Practising division	I think	My partner thinks
(m) I can solve a division problem, using counters, both as grouping and sharing.		
I explain to my partner what I am doing when I divide out the counters.		
I work well with my partner and share the work fairly.		

Self and peer assessment

Handling data

Learning objectives

	Lessons			
	17	**18**	**19**	**20**
Maths objectives				
organise data on a pictogram	●			
organise data on a Carroll diagram		●		
organise data on a Venn diagram			●	
organise data on a bar chart with intervals labelled in twos				●
Speaking and listening skills				
contribute to small-group discussion	●			
listen with sustained concentration		●	●	
explain and justify thinking				●
Personal skills				
work with others: discuss and agree ways of working	●			
improve learning and performance: reflect on learning		●		
work with others: work cooperatively with others			●	
organise work: plan ways to solve a problem				●

About these lessons

Lesson 17: Making a pictogram

(m) Organise data on a pictogram

Children draw a pictogram, recording collections of coloured counters, using a symbol to show two units. The work can be made more interesting by using found objects such as bottle tops and acorns.

Contribute to small-group discussion

Classroom technique: Rotating roles

Children rotate roles, taking turns at picking counters, saying the colour and adding to the tally. Experiencing all aspects of the work puts them in a strong position when they later need to discuss how to transfer this information to a pictogram.

Work with others: discuss and agree ways of working

The first part of the main activity provides children with a structure, whereas in the second part, groups are asked to find their own way of working together.

Lesson 18: A Carroll diagram

(m) Organise data on a Carroll diagram

Representing names and then numbers on a Carroll diagram helps children understand in a general way how these diagrams work.

Listen with sustained concentration

Classroom technique: Ticket to explain

Each child must repeat the number and explanation offered by the previous child as their 'ticket' allowing them to offer their own contribution.

Improve learning and performance: reflect on learning

Encouraging children to reflect on what they have learned in a lesson helps them take responsibility for their own learning and gives them an opportunity to think about themselves objectively.

Lesson 19: A Venn diagram

(m) Organise data on a Venn diagram

Children sort names onto a one-criterion Venn diagram. This way of sorting is similar to the Carroll diagram and requires children to focus properly on their work.

Listen with sustained concentration

Classroom technique: Devil's advocate

When children sort names onto a Venn diagram, they include one deliberate error for other children to spot. This version of 'Devil's advocate' requires children to explain how they know the name is in the wrong place.

Work with others: work cooperatively with others

Pairs of children share the task equally and so cooperate in order to achieve their aim.

Lesson 20: Bar charts

(m) Organise data on a bar chart with intervals labelled in twos

As many scientific instruments have scales which cannot be marked with every number because of limited space, they have intervals of 10, 20, 50 or more, only some of which are marked with numbers. Working with bar charts with intervals labelled in twos introduces children to this idea.

Explain and justify thinking

Classroom technique: One between two

Working in pairs, children share a pencil, taking turns to instruct each other what to write or draw on the bar chart. If the 'Writer' does not agree with an instruction, they challenge their partner to explain their reasoning.

Organise work: plan ways to solve a problem

Children need to display information on a bar chart where the vertical axis shows intervals marked in twos. They must plan together how to represent odd-number values such as 3 or 7.

Making a pictogram
Classroom technique: Rotating roles

Keep check
Tell the children that you will add up all the totals, using a calculator, and check the result against the number of children in the class to make sure that everybody votes just once.

Readability
Pictograms are much more effective if the symbols are equally spaced, so draw attention to that as the children draw the symbols.

Discuss and agrees ways of working
Suggest a mini-plenary in which the class discuss ways of sharing the work fairly and involving everyone equally.

Symbols
Children may understand the idea of a symbol standing for two things, but need support in using this idea when drawing a pictogram for themselves. It may help if, for each colour, they first work out how many symbols they need to use, then draw them, rather than starting to draw and then losing count.

Introduction

Ask each child in the class, in turn, to choose their favourite fruit from a given list. Make a tally of the results.

Count up the total for each fruit, scribe it and check if the total matches the number of voters.

apple	I I I	3
banana	I I I I I I	6
cherry	I I I I	4
pear	I I	2

Start to sketch a pictogram, with every two children being shown by a square. Volunteers continue the pictogram, drawing in the correct number of squares for each total. As odd totals occur, discuss the use of a half-square to show one person.

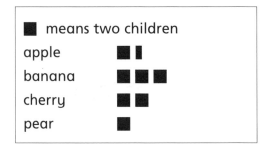

(m) *How many squares will you need to show 8?*

(m) *How can we check this pictogram is correct?*

Groups of three

Each group of children has a bag of coloured counters.

Child A picks five counters from the bag, Child B says the colours, and Child C makes a tally of these. After each turn, children rotate roles. This continues until they have picked 30 counters between them.

Groups then work together to show their results on a pictogram, using a symbol of their choice to stand for two occurrences of a particular colour.

(m) *You need to show there were 16 red counters. How many squares will that be?*

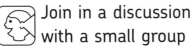
(m) *How many counters did you pick from the bag in all? So what is the overall total your pictogram should show?*

(s) *Do you agree with what Freddy just said? Why not?*

Support: Children work in mixed-ability groups, possibly using lined paper.

Extend: Children discuss the probability aspects of this activity: halfway through picking out counters, can they predict what the final numbers might look like and explain why?

Plenary

> **Deeper understanding**
> Introducing a symbol for 10 as well as one for 2 should deepen children's understanding of the pictogram.

Each group contributes their tally results, from which you construct a class pictogram. Collect in all the groups' numbers for one colour, total these on a calculator and put them on the pictogram.

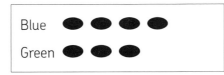

Continue with the other colours and involve all the class in checking that the pictogram shows the correct values for each colour.

(m) *Which colour of counter does the pictogram show most of? How many is that?*

(s) *Talk with your group about how many red counters you think were picked out of bags in the whole class.*

Assessment for learning

Can the children

(m) Record a quantity such as 12 counters on a pictogram?

(s) Tell their group how a number should be shown on the pictogram?

(☺) Show that they are sharing the work?

If not

(m) Use symbols regularly to represent different values. Show a value with the symbols and ask pairs to work out the value. Use pictograms to make graphs of interest to the children: merit points, milks drunk, and so on.

(s) Devise group activities where each member, in turn, says something about their work.

(☺) Observe the group working and suggest ways in which more passive children can contribute.

A Carroll diagram
Classroom technique: Ticket to explain

Learning objectives

(m) Maths
Organise data on
a Carroll diagram

Speaking and listening
'Listen well'
Listen with sustained
concentration

Personal skills
'Think about what you
have learned'
Improve learning and
performance: reflect on learning

(W) Words and phrases
set, sort, Carroll
diagram, represent, label,
title

(r) Resources
for each pair:
two 0–9 dice
copy of RS15
sticky notes

Tell your partner
Children who were not asked to
put their number on the diagram
turn to their neighbour and tell
them their number and where
on the diagram it belongs.

Sorting by two criteria
This last stage is the most
difficult and the most important
as you are supporting children in
the process of keeping two ideas
in mind simultaneously; in the
next part of the lesson, they will
have to do this for themselves.

Sticky notes
Sticking the numbers on rather
than writing them in allows
children to change their
minds later.

Introduction

Ask each child to choose a number under 200 and
write it down. Sketch a simple vertical Carroll diagram,
showing 'greater than 30' and 'not greater than 30'.
Invite a dozen or so children to say their number and
which side of the diagram it belongs in. Explain that
this is the basic principle of a Carroll diagram.

greater than 30	56 100 99 50
not greater than 30	17 2 12

Now sketch a horizontal Carroll diagram, showing 'even'
and 'not even' and work with the class to sort the same
numbers onto it.

even	not even
56 50 100 2 12	17 99

Draw a combined diagram, showing both descriptions
and their negatives. Work through the numbers again,
asking each time which side of the vertical line *and*
which side of the horizontal line the number should go.

Check the result by taking one box at a time and
looking at each number in turn – for example,
checking the numbers that are not greater than
30 and are even.

Repeat this for the other three boxes.

(m) *Tell us another number which could go in this part
of the diagram.*

(m) *What is the same about all these numbers?*

Pairs

Working in pairs, children share a copy of RS15. Child A
rolls the two 0–9 dice to make a two-digit number,
which Child B writes down on a small sticky note.
Both children then discuss where on the chart that
number should go, reach a decision and stick on the
sticky note.

Decision making

One child could take charge of the comparison with 30, while the other child decides whether the number is even or not. This makes the intellectual challenge easier, but, at the same time, gives the children a greater incentive to turn their thinking into speech to justify to their partner what they have done.

Making assessments

As you observe children, you may become aware that some are struggling with this work. Make a note of their names so that you can give them more support when this area of maths is revisited.

Ticket to explain

Each child must repeat the number and explanation offered by the previous child as their 'ticket' allowing them to offer their own contribution.

Discussion points

There are useful debates to be held about whether 0 is odd or even (arguably, zero is even because it is a multiple of 2) and where 30 should go (it is not greater than 30).

They repeat this until they have five or more numbers in each section of the diagram.

(m) *Is 37 greater than 30?*

(m) *Why does 67 belong in that part of the diagram?*

(☺) *What do you think you are learning about here?*

Support: Work with this group and change RS15 to read 'greater than 20' instead of 'greater than 30'.

Extend: Use three 0–9 dice and change RS15 to read 'greater than 300' instead of 'greater than 30'. Alternatively, children choose their own criteria.

Plenary

Collect in suggestions of numbers to go in each of the four areas, each time asking for an explanation. Use 'Ticket to explain' (p11) to ensure that children listen to each other.

Finally, ask children to spend a minute discussing with their partners what they have been learning about in this lesson, then open out a brief class discussion on this.

(👂) *Why did Asif think that 23 belongs here?*

(☺) *What have you learnt about sorting?*

(☺) *What did you find difficult, or easy, today?*

Assessment for learning

Can the children

(m) Find the correct place for a two-digit number on the Carroll diagram? For a three-digit number?

(👂) Listen to and repeat what another child has just said?

(☺) Say what they have been learning in the lesson?

If not

(m) Focus on sorting by just one criterion (for example, odd and even). Make sure children understand what odd and even numbers are.

(👂) Practise listening skills with the class, using games such as 'Simon says', where children repeat what the leader has said – but only if this is preceded by the words 'Simon says'.

(☺) Make a point of discussing with children the purpose of a lesson.

A Venn diagram
Classroom technique: Devil's advocate

Learning objectives

(m) Maths
Organise data on
a Venn diagram

Speaking and listening
'Listen well'
Listen with sustained
concentration

Personal skills
'Work cooperatively
with others'
Work with others: work
cooperatively with others

(W) Words and phrases
set, sort, Venn
diagram, intersection, label,
title

(r) Resources
display copy of RS16
for each pair:
copy of RS16
list of children in the class
Sticky notes

Introduction

Sketch a circle inside a rectangular border and label the circle 'Names containing the letter e'. Ask for a name – for example, Luke. Establish that 'Luke' contains the letter e and should be written inside the circle. Ask for another name that doesn't contain an e. Write it outside the circle. Continue this process with other names, including names with and without e.

Sketch a new circle inside a rectangular border and label the circle 'Names containing the letter a'. Repeat the sorting with the same names.

Display RS16. Label the circle 'Names containing the letter e'.

Add some more names, making one or more errors. Children show they have spotted an error with a 'thumbs down'. Ask for explanations about your errors.

(m) *What can you say about the names in this section of the diagram?*

(speaking icon) *Why does 'Mia' not belong in this section? Where should it go?*

Pairs

Children work in pairs with a class list and a copy of RS16. Child A writes down a name on a sticky note, and Child B places it in the appropriate section of the diagram, saying why it belongs there. After doing this a few times more, children change the criterion and re-sort the names.

When children have sorted a good number of names, stop the class and ask the children to add one more name, but to put it in the wrong section of their diagram. Pairs now swap sheets with another pair to spot the deliberate error, then agree and write a brief statement explaining why the name's position is incorrect and where the name should be placed.

Spot the error
It doesn't matter if pairs spot an unintentional error – the aim is to use their reasoning to clarify where a name does, and does not, belong.

What do the names in this section have in common? How do you know?

How are you sharing the work? Is it fair?

Support: Work with this group.

Extend: Children find at least two names for each part of the diagram.

Plenary

Choose a secret letter and start sorting the names of the class onto the diagram on RS16. Write each name in the appropriate section.

Ask the children to suggest what criterion you are choosing and what to label the circle.

Both 'Aaron' and 'Emma' are in the circle. What do the names have in common?

You say that what I have just written is incorrect. Why is that?

Agree with your partner which of you is going to write this name on the diagram.

Assessment for learning

Can the children

(m) Find the correct part of the Venn diagram to write a name in?

Identify an error and say why it is wrong?

Find a way of sharing work fairly?

If not

(m) Sort small-world objects into hoops, using one criterion. Then re-sort, using a different criterion.

Ask another child to find the error and explain it to this child, then ask them to repeat what they have just heard.

Stop the class for a mini-plenary where you discuss ways of working cooperatively.

Bar charts

Classroom technique: One between two

Learning objectives

(m) Maths
Organise data on a bar chart with intervals labelled in twos

Speaking and listening
'Explain what you think and why you think it'
Explain and justify thinking

Personal skills
'Plan ways to solve a problem'
Organise work: plan ways to solve a problem

(w) Words and phrases
represent, tally chart, bar chart, label, title, axis, axes, most popular, most common, least popular, least common

(r) Resources
display copies of RS17 and RS18
for each pair:
copy of RS18
ruler
RS19 (optional)

Tell your partner
Using this technique (p10), children turn to their partner and say which three pets they choose. Their partner repeats these and helps the child remember the choices.

An even number
Showing, for example, 4 fish is easy because the vertical axis shows a 4. This avoids pre-empting the issue of how to deal with showing an odd number such as 3.

One between two
One child has the pencil and is instructed by their partner what to write or draw, and where – no pointing allowed. After a while, they swap roles. The 'Writer' challenges any instruction they do not understand or disagree with.

RS18
The blank bar chart allows children to focus on using the scale marked in twos correctly. Children may want to write in the 'missing numbers': if they do, they need to write them lightly, so that they can rub them out later and try to manage without them.

Introduction

Display RS17 and ask children which three different pets from the list they would like, telling them that they must stick by their choices.

Make a tally on RS17 of the children's choices and discuss the results.

> Which animal was most popular?
> How many children chose a dog?

Display RS18. Choose an animal from the tally which had an even number of votes and remind children how to transfer this information to the bar chart.

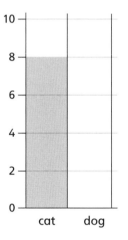

(m) *How do we show on a bar chart that 8 children chose a cat?*

(speaking) *Which pet was chosen most often? How do you know that?*

Pairs/Groups of four

Leave the tally on display for the class to see.

Pairs of children share a copy of RS18. They transfer the data from the tally chart to their bar chart, using 'One between two' (p8).

When pairs have completed their chart, they get together with another pair and compare charts, checking for any discrepancies and correcting these.

Tammy says that 5 will have to come halfway between 4 and 6. Do you agree? Why does she think that?

 You need to show '9 children', but there is no 9 on the axis here. What are you going to do about that?

Support: Children work in mixed-ability pairs, where a confident child supports their less confident partner. Remind the more confident child to question gently any unclear or inaccurate instructions.

Extend: Children work with RS19.

Plenary

Display RS18 again and complete the bar chart, with the help of the children. Children then answer some questions about it and ask some of their own.

(m) *How do we read a chart like this, with only even numbers?*

(m) *Can you finish off this sentence: 'More than 18 children in the class wanted a …'?*

(smiley) *How did you deal with the fact that this axis only showed even numbers? Did anyone else do it differently?*

Assessment for learning

Can the children

(m) Put data on the bar chart accurately?

(think) Explain how they know how high a bar should be drawn?

(smiley) Deal with only even numbers being shown on the vertical axis?

If not

(m) Highlight the horizontal lines on the chart with a marker so that they stand out as guides for the children.

(think) Ask children to show you instead, then offer an explanation for them to repeat back to you.

(smiley) Encourage pairs of children to stop their work and talk to another pair, sharing ideas about how they are solving the problem.

Self and peer assessment

Lesson 17: Making a pictogram	I think	My partner thinks
(m) I know how to record 12 counters on a pictogram.		
I tell my group what I think we need to do.		
I help make sure we are sharing our work.		

Lesson 18: A Carroll diagram	I think	My partner thinks
(m) I can put [ ] and [ ] in the correct place on a Carroll diagram.		
I listen carefully to what other children say.		
I can say what we have been learning in this lesson.		

Name _____

Lesson 19: A Venn diagram	I think	My partner thinks
(m) I can write a name in the correct part of the Venn diagram.		
(face) I can spot a name that is in the wrong part of the diagram and say why it is wrong.		
(face) I share the work fairly with my partner.		

Lesson 20: Bar charts	I think	My partner thinks
(m) I work accurately when I show information on a bar chart.		
(face) I can explain how I work out where to draw a bar on the chart.		
(face) I can work out with my partner how to show 3 and 5 on the chart.		

Measures

Learning objectives

	Lessons			
	21	**22**	**23**	**24**
Maths objectives				
solve simple problems about weight	●			
measure and compare lengths, using standard units		●		
know the relationship between minutes and hours			●	
make and describe right-angled turns				●
Speaking and listening skills				
explain and justify thinking	●			
share and discuss ideas and reach consensus		●		
reach a common understanding with a partner			●	
use precise language to explain ideas or give information				●
Personal skills				
organise work: plan and manage a group task	●			
improve learning and performance: assess learning progress		●		
work with others: overcome difficulties and recover from mistakes			●	
improve learning and performance: take pride in work				●

About these lessons

Lesson 21: Comparing weights

Solve simple problems about weight

Children compare the weights of three or more objects, using a balance. This involves not only putting different pairs of objects in the balance but interpreting correctly what children see.

Explain and justify thinking

Classroom technique: Think, pair, share

Children think about a problem as individuals, then discuss their ideas with a partner. Finally, they share ideas with another pair. This gives all children an opportunity to think about a problem and to express their ideas and justify their conclusions.

Organise work: plan and manage a group task

Groups of four children have the task of putting objects in order of weight, using one balance. They share the responsibility of completing the task and of ensuring that they do so as equal partners.

Lesson 22: Measuring length

Measure and compare lengths, using standard units

Pairs of children measure various body parts, then join with other pairs to compare measurements and answer the question: "Does the person with the smallest head also have the smallest feet?"

Share and discuss ideas and reach consensus

Classroom technique: Peer tutoring

Children who show competence at measuring and recording are given the title 'Measuring Tutors'. These children share their knowledge and understanding with any other children who are having difficulties with the task of measuring.

Improve learning and performance: assess learning progress

In the plenary, groups discuss what they have been learning and how their skills in this area are improving.

Lesson 23: Timelines

Know the relationship between minutes and hours

Children make jumps of 15, 30, 45 or 60 minutes (or their equivalents as fractions of an hour) on a timeline. Discussing the size of each jump reinforces the equivalents such as $\frac{1}{4}$ hour and 15 minutes or 1 hour and 60 minutes.

Reach a common understanding with a partner

Classroom technique: Tell your partner

In the introduction and plenary, the technique 'Tell your partner' (p10) is used to encourage children to discuss the problems and questions you pose and to agree answers.

Work with others: overcome difficulties and recover from mistakes

Each pair works independently, but on the same task – drawing jumps on the timeline – as everybody else. After each stage, you draw the jumps on your own timeline. If children have had difficulties or made mistakes, they can correct their jumps to match yours.

Lesson 24: Making turns

Make and describe right-angled turns

Children instruct each other to make one, two or three right-angled turns (or their equivalents as fractions of a turn) on a dial marked with compass points. Discussing the size of each turn reinforces the equivalents such as $\frac{1}{2}$ turn and one right angle or $\frac{3}{4}$ turn and three right angles.

Use precise language to explain ideas or give information

Classroom technique: Rotating roles

Children work in threes, taking a turn at each role. First, they choose a card showing instructions about making a turn; then they interpret and act on the instruction given by another child. Finally, they check the move has been carried out correctly.

Improve learning and performance: take pride in work

Groups discuss how well they have worked in the lesson, in terms of personal and language skills as well as mathematical ones. Each group also agrees a joint statement about how proud they are of their achievement.

Comparing weights

Classroom technique: Think, pair, share

Learning objectives

(m) Maths
Solve simple problems about weight

Speaking and listening
'Explain what you think and why you think it'
Explain and justify thinking

Personal skills
'Plan and manage a group task'
Organise work: plan and manage a group task

(w) Words and phrases
balance, scales, compare, estimate, check, weigh, balances, heavier/lighter, heaviest/lightest, predict

(r) Resources
three packets (A, B, C) containing different weights of sand
display balance
for each group:
three objects of different weights (bag of conkers or shells, carton of acorns, apples, stick of cubes)
balance

Packets of sand
When comparing weights by hand, it is easy to be confused by the different shapes of the object. Using packets of sand helps avoid this problem.

Think, pair, share
Children think as individuals, then discuss their ideas with a partner before sharing ideas with another pair. Keep the timing sharp on this procedure.

Estimating
To keep this moving, time it: give Child A in each group one minute to make their comparisons and jot them down, then move on to Child B, and so on. Use 'Think, pair, share' (p10): as individuals, children check what they have recorded before comparing and discussing this with a partner. At the end, all four children share ideas and agree a common estimate.

Introduction

Show the children three packets (A, B, C) containing different weights of sand. Ask a child to hold one packet in each hand and estimate which is heavier. Repeat this with other children as a check, then write up the response, using 'heavier than' and 'lighter than'.

Repeat this with a different pair of packets, writing up responses as before. Finally, use the other combination of two packets and repeat.

We think that ...	
B is heavier than A	A is lighter than B
C is heavier than A	A is lighter than C
B is heavier than C	C is lighter than B

Check the comparisons, using a balance. Compare a pair of objects at a time and ask for predictions as to how the balance will behave, based on the earlier comparisons.

Work with the class to record the order of the packets.

Weight of the three packets
heaviest to lightest
B   C   A

(m) *You say that B will go down and A will go up. What does that mean about their weights?*

(speaking) *Which of these three is heaviest? Can you explain why you think that?*

(speaking) *This packet is the middle weight. Does that match with what we worked out earlier?*

Groups of four

Give each group of four children a balance and three objects to put in order of weight. Groups briefly test the feel of the objects, agree an estimate of the order of weights and put the three objects in order of weight on the balance.

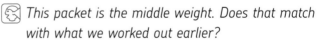

(speaking) *Why do you think the heaviest thing will be the stick of cubes?*

Is anyone in the group doing more/less than the others? How can you share out the work better?

Support: Children work in pairs.

Extend: Children order four or five objects by weight.

Plenary

Take one group's set of three objects and record them in order of weight.

Weight of the three objects
heaviest to lightest
bag of conkers   marker pen   stick of cubes

Showing the class one more object, ask how to work out, as quickly as possible, where to put this in the order. Children instruct you to put it on a balance with another object from the set.

Repeat with one or more other objects.

Sean wants me to compare the book with the bag of conkers. Does anyone disagree?

The book is heavier than the bag of conkers. So what else do I know about its weight?

Where do we need to put the apple in this list of weights? How do we know it belongs there?

Assessment for learning

Can the children

Use the balance to compare the weights of two or three objects?

Explain what they can tell about the objects' weights from the position of the balance pans?

Find a way to keep all members of the group involved in the task?

If not

Do more work on feeling the pull of light and heavy objects such as empty and full shopping bags and discussing what that means about their weights.

Give children opportunities to explore the use of balances in their free time and encourage them to talk about what they find out.

Stop the class for a mini-plenary and discuss ways of sharing the group task.

Measuring length
Classroom technique: Peer tutoring

Learning objectives

 Maths
Measure and compare lengths, using standard units

Speaking and listening
'Share ideas and reach agreement'
Share and discuss ideas and reach consensus

Personal skills
'Assess your progress in learning'
Improve learning and performance: assess learning progress

W Words and phrases
measure, length, compare, estimate, longer, shorter, longest, shortest, metre, centimetre, reason

r Resources
display copy of RS20
for each pair:
two copies of RS20
ruler
tape measure showing centimetres
and millimetres
for each group:
copy of RS21

Tell your partner
Using this technique (p10), involve all children by asking questions or requesting predictions about the measurements. Children then discuss the matter with a neighbour.

Peer tutoring
Take note of any children who are showing competence at measuring and recording and write up their names on the board, under the heading 'Measuring Tutors'. Any pairs who are having difficulties consult them and only turn to you as a last resort.

Organisation
Children need to be well organised in this activity. Some structure is provided by the two resource sheets, but there is plenty for children to do themselves, particularly ordering. Observe how each group is progressing and intervene as necessary.

Introduction

Display a copy of RS20. Discuss and demonstrate how to do each measurement with several volunteers, talking about where each part of the body is and exactly where to start and end the measurement.

Identify and discuss issues such as using a flexible measuring instrument (for example, a tape measure), using the same side all the way round and measuring from 0 on a scale, not from 1.

m *Why does it matter that everybody measures feet in the same way?*

(speaking icon) *Do you think Rudi's head measurement will be more than Jacob's? Tell your partner what you think.*

Pairs/Groups of six

Pairs of children complete a copy of RS20. The child who is being measured directs the activity; the other does the measuring and writes down the results. Children then swap roles.

After having completed both sets of measurements, pairs get together with two other pairs. Write up the question: "Is your height the same length as your span?" The group task is to fill in the charts on RS21 as a way of answering this. On the first chart, children compile a list of measurements under each child's name; on the second chart, they put the measurements in order, with the child's name or initial in brackets.

Measurements in order

largest ⟶

Height	50 cm (F)	48 cm (J)
Span	27 cm (J)	26 cm (S)

The group then discuss and agree an answer to the question posed.

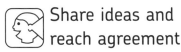
(m) *How does that tape measure show you the distance around Lara's head?*

(face) *Which head measurement is the largest? Do you all agree?*

(smiley) *Are you getting better at measuring accurately?*

Support: Children do the measurements on RS20 with adult support, then work in a group of four instead of six, so that there are fewer items to put in order.

Extend: Children order all the measurements and see what conclusions, if any, can be drawn from this.

Is there a relationship?
You will probably find that there is some correlation between head and foot size but nothing like a perfect match.

Plenary

Groups report back briefly on their answer to your question. They then discuss what they have been learning and how their skills in this area are improving.

(m) *Who in your group had the biggest head measurement? And the smallest?*

(face) *What answer to the question I wrote up did your group decide on?*

(smiley) *Tell your group one thing you must watch out for when you are measuring accurately.*

(smiley) *Was there anything in today's lesson that you found really easy? Or really difficult?*

1, 2, 3, 4, 5, 6
Children in a group number themselves 1 to 6, then decide, with the roll of a dice, which of them reports back to the class.

Assessment for learning

Can the children

(m) Measure a body part, using centimetres?

(face) Make a comment or suggestion to their group when discussing the question posed?

(smiley) Name one thing they have found easy or difficult in the lesson?

If not

(m) Consider whether a peer tutor could teach the child how to use and read the tape measure.

(face) Make a suggestion yourself and ask the child whether they agree or disagree, and why.

(smiley) Ask the child's partner for an assessment of what the child found easy or difficult and see if the child agrees.

Timelines

Classroom technique: Tell your partner

Tell your partner
Before you take comments from the class, pairs discuss what they notice about the timeline.

Introduction

Display RS22. Ask children what they notice about the timeline – for example, "It is divided into periods of 15 minutes"; "It covers the day from 8 o'clock in the morning to 8 o'clock at night."

Circle one time on the line. Pairs read the time to each other and agree where a jump of 30 minutes (or 15, 45 or 60 minutes) forwards from there would land.

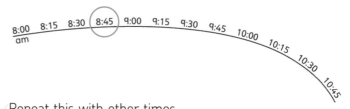

Making links
Use this introduction to make the links between the numerical time intervals (15, 30, 45 and 60 minutes) and their common names (quarter of an hour, half an hour, three quarters of an hour and hour).

Repeat this with other times.

(m) *We've got to 11:45. What is the other way of saying 11:45?*

(m) *Where will a jump of 30 minutes take me? Discuss this with your partner.*

(☺) *Have I made a mistake? How can I put it right?*

Pairs/Whole class

Play a class game, with children working in pairs to make jumps forwards in time from 8:00 am. Pairs work with a copy of RS22 and mark any ten target times on the timeline. Display your own copy of RS22 for the class to see.

Pick a time period at random from your copy of RS23 (mark the time so you know you have used it), read it out and write the time period on the board. Pairs draw a jump of that amount from 8:00 am. If they hit one of their targets, they score a point and take a counter.

Recover from mistakes
Children need to stay alert for mistakes and correct them. Drawing your own jumps supports children in this, but requires them to pay close attention or they may not notice that their jumps are different to yours.

Draw that jump on your copy of RS22, as a check.

Continue until everybody reaches 8:00 pm.

Discuss children's point scores with the class.

🗣 *Talk with your partner about why 30 minutes is called 'half an hour'.*

😊 *Why do you need to check your work?*

Support: Children pencil in their jumps lightly and check them carefully against the jumps you draw on your display copy of the line.

Extend: Pairs of children play the game against each other.

Plenary

Tell your partner
Use this technique (p10) again.

Display a clean copy of RS22 and ask volunteers to mark the times of the school day on the timeline. Ask children questions such as the length of a lesson or the amount of dinner time there is.

Ⓜ *How many minutes long is dinner time? How many hours?*

Making links again
Relating the pattern of the school day to the time intervals of 15, 30, 45 and 60 minutes will help deepen children's understanding of time in general.

🗣 *Numeracy starts at about 9:15 am and lasts an hour. Tell your partner where we should draw the jump to.*

Assessment for learning

Can the children

Ⓜ Say how many minutes are equivalent to $\frac{1}{4}$, $\frac{1}{2}$, $\frac{3}{4}$ and 1 hour?

🗣 Agree with their partner where a jump of, for example, 30 minutes will take them to on the timeline?

😊 Spot any errors they make in drawing jumps and self-correct them?

If not

Ⓜ Do some work on basic fractions in relation to shape and number before returning to the timeline as children may not be comfortable with these fractions.

🗣 Try some different pairings of children. For example, put together quieter or more passive children and encourage them to experiment with a more lively style of working.

😊 Check if children have visual or perceptual difficulties. Have a blitz on checking work against correct answers and going back over the work to correct errors.

Making turns

Classroom technique: Rotating roles

Learning objectives

(m) Maths
Make and describe right-angled turns

Speaking and listening
'Use precise language when talking'
Use precise language to explain ideas or give information

Personal skills
'Take pride in your work'
Improve learning and performance: take pride in work

(w) Words and phrases
clockwise, anticlockwise, compass point, North, South, East, West, N, S, E, W, whole turn, half turn, quarter turn, angle, right angle, correct

(r) Resources
display dial with rotating arrow made from RS24
for each group:
dial with rotating arrow made from RS24
24 cards cut from RS25
counters

Compass points
The four points around the circle are labelled North, South, East and West, but keep the main focus on turning rather than on the compass directions.

Right angles
If children have difficulty understanding that right-angled turns are the same as ¼ turns, organise a practical demonstration: ask children to stand up and turn through different amounts, using both kinds of description.

Rotating roles
Children take a turn at each role: choosing a card and giving instructions (supported by having these written on the card); interpreting and acting on the instructions; and checking the move has been carried out correctly.

Direction
In this game, one move away from North can often be followed by a move which returns the arrow to North and so scores a counter. You may want to point this out to children.

The end of the game
If all moves were made correctly, the last one will end on North (for Support, the game will end on South). You can use this to check whether a group has made all moves correctly.

Introduction

Display the dial made from RS24 and the first twelve cards cut from of RS25. Starting with the arrow pointing to North, ask a volunteer to choose one card and move the arrow according to the instructions.

Collect in instructions which would move the arrow to North.

(m) *Face the window. Now move through a ¼ turn.*

**** *What command could you choose to move the arrow to North?*

Groups of three

Groups of three children play a game to win counters. They have a dial made from RS24 and 24 cards cut from RS25. The group share three cards, with the remaining cards placed face down on the table.

Child A points the arrow to North, chooses one of the cards, reads it out and instructs Child B to move the arrow around that amount. Child C observes and checks that the correct move is made.

They replace the used card from the pack, and Child B has a turn. If their move takes the pointer to North, they win a counter for the group. Child C has a turn next.

Children keep playing like this until all cards are used up.

(m) *Tell me about that turn you have just made.*

**** *A ¼ turn will get you back to North. But which way, clockwise or anticlockwise?*

**** *Are you all doing well? Are you managing to understand each other and to win lots of counters?*

Support: Use 12 clockwise cards.

Extend: Have five cards visible at a time to choose from.

Plenary

Groups discuss how well they have fulfilled the task set. Take suggestions and write them up to provide a prompt for groups who are stuck.

Things to be proud of
– We understood the task.
– We listened to each other well.
– We worked hard.

Each group agrees a joint statement about how proud they are of their achievement: "We are proud that ..."

Finally, organise the class into three teams and play a competitive version of the game, using a display copy of the dial and cards from two copies of RS25 so that there are enough for each child to have one card. Within each team, each player has one turn to play a card after discussion with a partner from their team.

Instead of winning counters for the class, teams keep those they win. The winning team is the one with most counters at the end.

Assessment

This game provides an opportunity for you to see how well children have understood the ideas introduced in this lesson.

(m) *You asked me to make one right-angled turn clockwise. Do you mean like this?*

Tell me exactly what move I should make next.

What did you do particularly well today?

Assessment for learning

Can the children

(m) Make turns of one or more right angles, either clockwise or anticlockwise, as instructed?

Accurately describe the turn they have just made?

Find some achievement to be proud of?

If not

(m) Do similar activities on a giant clock face chalked on the floor, where children move their own bodies through one or more right-angled turns.

Ask another child to suggest a description and, if the child agrees with it, ask them to repeat it.

Give children some positive feedback yourself.

Self and peer assessment

Lesson 21: Comparing weights	I think	My partner thinks
(m) I can use the balance to compare the weights of ☐ objects.		
(🗣) I can explain what I know about the weights of two objects when I see the position of the balance pans.		
(☺) I help make sure everyone is involved in the group task.		

Lesson 22: Measuring length	I think	My partner thinks
(m) I can measure parts of my partner's body, using centimetres.		
(🗣) I listen to what the others in my group say and tell them if I don't agree.		
(☺) I can say what I found easy or difficult in the lesson.		

Name _____

Lesson 23: Timelines	I think	My partner thinks
(m) I can say how many minutes are the same as ¼ hour, ½ hour, ¾ hour and 1 hour.		
I listen to what my partner says and think about whether I agree with them.		
I look for errors in my work and correct them.		

Lesson 24: Making turns	I think	My partner thinks
(m) I can make turns of one or more right angles, either clockwise or anticlockwise.		
I can describe a turn I have just made.		
I can say something I did in the lesson that I am proud of.		

Self and peer assessment

Shape and space

Learning objectives

	Lessons			
	25	26	27	28
Maths objectives				
work with one or two lines of symmetry	●			
name and describe 2D shapes		●		
recognise and use compass directions: N, S, E, W			●	
describe position using coordinates				●
Speaking and listening skills				
use precise languge to explain ideas or give information	●			
listen with sustained concentration		●		
listen and follow instructions accurately			●	
reach a common understanding with a partner				●
Personal skills				
work with others: overcome difficulties and recover from mistakes	●			
work with others: show awareness and understanding of others' needs		●		
improve learning and performance: critically evaluate own work			●	
work with others: work cooperatively with others				●

About these lessons

Lesson 25: Working with symmetry

(m) Work with one or two lines of symmetry

One child makes a symmetrical pattern and describes it to their partner, who colours one the same. The task focuses children both on symmetry and on describing position.

Use precise language to explain ideas or give information

Classroom technique: Barrier game

The child describing their grid and the child drawing one the same cannot see each other's work. This means the 'Describer' must turn their thought processes into words without using gestures or pointing.

Work with others: overcome difficulties and recover from mistakes

Children can find it hard to listen closely enough to their partner to put their instructions into practice. The 'Listener' is encouraged to deal with this by asking questions to clarify exactly what was meant. They are also asked to check their work for errors and put these right.

Lesson 26: Describing 2D shapes

(m) Name and describe 2D shapes

Children describe one shape from a sheet of shapes so their partner can identify it and put a counter on it. They are encouraged to use a wide variety of language in describing the shapes, including (but not exclusively) the conventional vocabulary of shape.

Listen with sustained concentration

Classroom technique: Barrier game

Children work with a barrier between them and therefore need to rely on verbal communication. The 'Speaker' must describe the shapes adequately, and the 'Listener' must ask clarifying questions as necessary.

Work with others: show awareness and understanding of others' needs

The 'Speaker' must think about what information their partner needs to provide a description that identifies one, and only one, of the shapes.

Lesson 27: Compass directions

(m) Recognise and use compass directions: N, S, E, W

Children follow a route on a grid of letters, using the four points of the compass, to spell out a name. The activity is, to a certain extent, self-correcting, as any result which does not give the name of someone in the class must be incorrect and needs checking.

Listen and follow instructions accurately

Classroom technique: Barrier game

Pairs sit back to back with their partner and describe the route marked on their sheet. Their partner must listen carefully to draw the route on their own clean grid and work out the name.

Improve learning and performance: critically evaluate own work

In the plenary, children focus on the maths and speaking and listening objectives of the lesson, thinking about how they have achieved each objective.

Lesson 28: Coordinates

(m) Describe position using coordinates

Working in groups of four, one pair of children marks on a grid a square where the ant lives. The other pair must identify that square by saying the coordinates of various squares in turn. As a help, they are told how many steps away from home that square is.

Reach a common understanding with a partner

Classroom technique: Talking partners

Pairs work as a team, discussing what they know and how to make use of this information to work out the answer as quickly and efficiently as possible.

Work with others: work cooperatively with others

Pairs of children share the task of finding where the ant lives and need to cooperate to achieve their aim.

Working with symmetry
Classroom technique: Barrier game

Working with symmetry
Classroom technique: Barrier game

Learning objectives

(m) Maths
Work with one or two lines of symmetry

Speaking and listening
'Use precise language when talking'
Use precise language to explain ideas or give information

Personal skills
'Get over difficulties and mistakes'
Work with others: overcome difficulties and recover from mistakes

(w) Words and phrases
symmetrical, line of symmetry, fold, match, check, mirror line, reflection, pattern, position, over, under, above, below, between

(r) Resources
2 × 4, 4 × 4 and 6 × 6 squared grids coloured pens or pencils

Position
Here, you are modelling to the children how to turn what you can see into words, accurately and unambiguously. Your vocabulary will probably include nouns such as 'corner', 'diagonal', 'side', 'edge', 'row' and 'column' and adjectives such as 'left', 'right', 'top', 'bottom' and 'centre'.

Using symmetry
Optional: Only describe the left half of the grid. As long as children understand that the grid is symmetrical, they can fill in the reflected half to match.

Overcome difficulties
If children find it difficult to use words without the support of gestures, reassure them that practice will make it easier. As children may find it hard to listen closely enough to their partner to put their instructions into practice, encourage the 'Listener' to ask questions to clarify exactly what was meant.

Introduction

You need a 4 × 4 grid coloured in with a symmetrical pattern using three or four colours. Keep the grid hidden from the children.

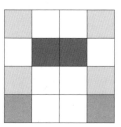

Give each pair of children a blank 4 × 4 grid and ask them to fold it in half (the fold line is the axis of symmetry). Describe part of your pattern. Pairs discuss and agree which squares they need to colour in on the blank grid. Continue this process until children's grids are complete.

Finally, children check that their grids are symmetrical, asking you questions if necessary. Display your grid for children to check for any discrepancies between your and their grids.

(m) *The squares in the top row go green, blue, blue, green.*

(m) *On the left side, the bottom corner square is red. The square next to that is blue. You can work out if the same squares are on the other side.*

(☺) *I wonder why there are blanks on your grid and none on mine. How can we put that right?*

Pairs

Children do the same activity, with a barrier such as a large book between them. They put their names on their grids so that you can see the original and its copy when you talk to the pair.

After each game, the 'Listener' checks their work for symmetry, asks questions to help them correct any obvious errors and compares grids with the 'Describer', as a final check. Children then swap roles.

(ⓜ) Use precise language when talking

lesson **25**

(m) *How does the symmetry help you spot errors?*

(📧) *How can you describe where that square is?*

(☺) *Can you see any squares which are wrong on the copy? What can you do to correct them?*

Support: Use a 2 × 4 grid and only two colours (children can move on to a larger grid and more colours as appropriate). One child tells the other how to move from a certain square to one that they want coloured in: "Start in the bottom left corner – that's red. Go sideways one square. Colour that blue."

Extend: Use a 6 × 6 grid and up to five colours. Work with two folds, at right angles (two lines of symmetry).

Plenary

Present a 6 × 6 coloured grid and an empty 6 × 6 grid.

Children choose part of the coloured grid and describe to you how to fill in the empty one so it is the same. Discuss with the class the different techniques they use and suggest that next time they do this activity, they try out a new technique.

(📧) *Tell me which squares to colour red.*

(☺) *Did you mean me to colour this square blue? Have I got it wrong?*

Assessment for learning

Can the children

(m) Create a symmetrical pattern on their own grid using one or two lines of symmetry?

(📧) Describe the position of a particular square well enough to identify it?

(☺) Deal with the constraints of hearing the description but not seeing the pattern described?

If not

(m) Do work arranging objects either side of a mirror line. Provide mirrors and help children use them to see what a real reflection looks like. Compare this to their arrangement.

(📧) Do more work as in the introduction, modelling, and getting articulate children to model, useful language.

(☺) Ask children to lift the barrier after each of the 'Listener's' squares are identified, but before they are coloured, as a check.

Describing 2D shapes
Classroom technique: Barrier game

Learning objectives

m Maths
Name and describe
2D shapes

Speaking and listening
'Listen well'
Listen with sustained
concentration

Personal skills
'Think about what
other people need'
Work with others: show
awareness and understanding
of others' needs

W Words and phrases
curved, straight, corner,
vertex, vertices, right-angled,
semicircle, triangle, square,
rectangle, pentagon,
hexagon, octagon,
position, symmetrical

r Resources
display copy
of RS26
for each pair:
two copies of RS26
coloured counters

Tell your partner
Children turn to their partner and
say as many different names as
they can think of: 'chimney',
'six-sided', 'roof', and so on.
Don't expect them to distinguish
between describing words
(adjectives) and names (nouns).
The purpose of this is to
encourage children to observe
the features of the shapes
and making links between
these features and the
mathematical name.

Limitations
Emphasise that the mathematical
name of a shape does not
necessarily tell you a lot about
the shape. For example, there
are two hexagons on the sheet,
but 'upside-down L' identifies
which of the two you are
referring to better than
just 'hexagon'.

Short cuts
Allow for short cuts such as:
"Put red counters on the
two half-circles."

Describing shapes
Encourage the child to whom
their partner describes the
shapes to ask clarifying
questions: "Do you mean the
triangle above the square?"

Introduction
Display RS26. Children find names to describe the
various shapes.

Collect in suggestions and make sure to establish the
mathematical names as well.

Invite children, one at a time, to choose a shape and
describe it. The class then instruct you which shape
to put a coloured counter on. Discuss any ambiguities.
Continue this until each shape has one counter on it.

m *Can you explain the difference between these
two semicircles?*

**Lisa said to put a red counter on a triangle.
Which kind of triangle did she say?**

Pairs
Each pair of children works with a copy of RS26.
Children sit back to back or with a barrier between
them. The 'Speaker' describes a shape to the 'Listener',
places a coloured counter on it and tells the 'Listener'
to do the same.

The pair continues like this until all shapes have a
counter on.

At the end, children compare sheets and note any
discrepancies. They swap roles and repeat the activity,
aiming for a complete match.

Tell your partner which of the L-shapes to put her counter on.

You need to explain clearly which shape you mean so that your partner understands you.

Support: Use half of the number of shapes only.
Extend: Children draw up their own sheet of shapes.

Plenary

Efficient questioning
Work with the children to keep track of how many or how few questions are asked in each game and note those questions which eliminate several shapes at once.

Play a guessing game with the class. Display RS26 again (or display a selection of shapes from another source) and choose one shape in secret. Give children one clue and encourage them to ask questions to identify your chosen shape.

Play again, inviting a child to choose the shape in secret.

The shape I have chosen doesn't have any right angles.

What question would help you narrow down the possible choices?

Assessment for learning

Can the children

Name and/or describe the shapes on the sheet?

Pay attention to their partner's instructions to identify the shape in question?

Attempt to give an adequate description, rather than rely on their partner to ask questions?

If not

Have a blitz on the properties of shapes and the language to describe these. Try sorting activities and shapes in feely bags (which appeal to the sense of touch rather than sight).

Do further work on listening to, and acting on, descriptions.

Discuss what it is like to be the 'Listener' and what the person in that role needs from their partner.

Compass directions
Classroom technique: Barrier game

Learning objectives

(m) Maths
Recognise and use compass directions: N, S, E, W

Speaking and listening
'Listen and follow instructions'
Listen and follow instructions accurately

Personal skills
'Evaluate your own work'
Improve learning and performance: critically evaluate own work

(w) Words and phrases
compass point, North, South, East, West, N, S, E, W, horizontal, vertical, grid, row, column, position, route, check

(r) Resources
compass
two display copies of RS27
for each child:
two copies of RS27

Introduction

Display RS27 and show the class how to use a compass to find North. Discuss how, on maps, North is shown at the top.

Ask a volunteer to leave the room. Choose the name of a child in the class, find the first (capital) letter of their name on RS27 and circle it.

With the class, find the second letter and circle that, and so on, ending with a full stop. Join the letters in sequence with a route drawn horizontally and vertically. Finally, invite the class to help you turn this route into a sequence of instructions, using the points of the compass, and ask for the number of steps to be taken (do not allow the words 'up', 'down', 'left' and 'right'). End the route with the full stop.

A few pointers
Ending the route on the full stop provides an immediate check on whether the route has been accurately given and received. The route can cross over itself, but keep it simple. Commonly repeated letters appear twice on the grid to minimise repeated visits to one square.

Start with B. Go East 4 squares and South 1 square. Stop and circle that letter.

Call the volunteer back in and display a new copy of RS27. Keep the original hidden. Help the class repeat the series of instructions, including the full stop, so that the volunteer can draw the route and work out the name of the child.

(m) *The next letter is four steps away – in which direction?*

Compass points
If you think children can manage without the compass points drawn on RS27, cut them off.

Their own names
This means children's names will be spelled correctly: when other children later interpret the name, they will not need to know how it is spelled as they will discover this by following the route.

Repeat to yourself what the last instruction was to help you remember it.

Pairs

Give each child a copy of RS27. Working alone and using their own name, children colour in the relevant squares on the grid and draw the route. Collect in the sheets and redistribute them. Each child needs a filled-in sheet and a clean one. Working in pairs, children sit with their back to their partner and

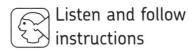
The need for accuracy
This activity requires accurate description and careful listening: one error, however slight, may make the name unintelligible. One possible source of error here is that children count the square that they are on as 'one' instead of counting the first square they move to. As with a number line, remind children to count steps, not squares.

describe the route marked on their sheet. Their partner draws it on their own clean grid and works out the name. Children then swap roles and work with their partner's name.

 *Do you need to check that you heard that instruction correctly?*

With this second map, are you working more quickly and easily?

Support: Children use names that only have three or four letters.

Extend: Children use both first and second names. Allow diagonal moves: North-East, South-East, South-West or North-West.

Plenary

Remind children of the maths and speaking and listening objectives of the lesson: write them up and briefly discuss what they mean and how they relate to what the children have been doing.

> Recognise and use compass directions: N, S, E, W
>
> Listen and follow instructions.

Self-evaluation
Encourage children to think about whether there is room for improvement, and in what way, and to acknowledge if they have achieved more than asked for – perhaps using all eight compass directions.

Give children a minute to think about how they have achieved each objective, then another two minutes to share these thoughts with their partner.

m *The whiteboard is to the North of this room. What is to the East?*

What do you think stops you listening well?

How hard did you work today?

Assessment for learning

Can the children

m Use the four compass directions to describe a route?

Recreate on their own grid the route described by a partner?

Name one thing they have done well and another where there is room for improvement?

If not

m Work on compass directions, using a grid chalked on the floor or outside in the playground.

Do work on listening to, and acting on, descriptions of compass.

Work with the class to draw up a short list of possible achievements and ask children to assess themselves on each one. Make sure you give children realistic but gentle assessments of their achievement.

Coordinates

Classroom technique: Talking partners

Learning objectives

ⓜ Maths
Describe position using coordinates

Speaking and listening
'Reach an understanding with your partner'
Reach a common understanding with a partner

Personal skills
'Work cooperatively with others'
Work with others: work cooperatively with others

ⓦ Words and phrases
grid, row, column, horizontal, vertical, position, work out, check

ⓡ Resources
display copies of RS28
RS29
for each group:
two copies of RS28

Numbers of steps away

Writing the number of steps a square is away from the ant's home allows children to look back at and use all the information they have.
If the other children are having difficulties working out how many steps a square is away from the ant's home, help them correct any errors. Otherwise, the searchers' task of locating the ant will be impossible.

Strategy

If children simply guess the location of the ant's home, rather than using the information they have acquired, remind them to discuss what they know with their partner and work out the answer as quickly and efficiently as possible. One strategy is to colour in all possible homes for each answer: this will soon narrow down the range of possible squares.

Introduction

Display the grid on RS28. Ask two volunteers to leave the room while the class choose and mark on the grid a square where an ant lives.

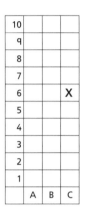

The volunteers come back in and sit at the front of the class with a copy of RS28 and their back to the display copy. Their shared task is to work out where the ant lives. They do this by saying the coordinates of a square and being told how many steps away from the ant's home that square is.

> B3 is 4 steps away from home.
> A7 is 3 steps away from home.

ⓜ *How do you find where C3 is?*

ⓜ *Could the ant be at A1? Why not?*

Agree with your partner which square to ask about next.

What could go wrong when playing the game?

Groups of four

Children play this game as two teams of two. Both teams need a copy of RS28, either to remind them of where the ant is or, if they are the searchers, to record the information they are given. Encourage pairs to discuss which square to ask about, so that they get useful information.

(m) *Is there a square in the C column which could be the answer?*

(☺) *Look back at the first square you asked about and the answer you got. Discuss with your partner how that fits with what you have just been told.*

(☺) *Why must you give an accurate answer to the other team's question?*

Support: Use the smaller grid on RS29.

Extend: Use the larger grid on RS29.

Plenary

Systematic working

Use children's suggestions to identify all possible homes that would fit each answer you give: "You've guessed A7, and I gave you 3 as an answer. Let's find every square that is three steps away from A7. If I go three steps straight down the A column, I get to A4. I'll colour that in. Suppose I go down two steps and then across one step. I get to B5 ..."

Display the grid on RS28 again and choose a home for the ant yourself. Challenge the class to find it, asking four questions or less. Collect in suggestions for the first square to ask about and take a vote on which suggestion should be used. Mark on the grid the number of steps that square is away from the ant's home.

Continue this until the class have found the ant's home.

(m) *When the ant was on C10, was it easier to find than when it was on B5? Why?*

(☺) *Talk to your a partner about which of the two suggestions you think are most useful.*

Assessment for learning

Can the children

(m) Describe the position of a square, using coordinates?

(☺) Discuss and agree with a partner the choices to make in the game?

(☺) Share decision making, rather than take a back seat or make all the decisions?

If not

(m) Play the game again, using peer tutors (p8) to work with and advise children having difficulties.

(☺) Make an obviously bad suggestion yourself and ask the child whether they think it is a good or bad choice, and why.

(☺) Make sure children take turns at decision making and always explain their reasons to their partner, as a step on the way to joint decision making.

Self and peer assessment

Lesson 25: Working with symmetry	I think	My partner thinks
(m) I can make a symmetrical pattern using one line/two lines of symmetry.		
I can describe the position of a square well enough so my partner knows which one I mean.		
I keep trying even if I get frustrated by an activity or find it difficult.		

Lesson 26: Describing 2D shapes	I think	My partner thinks
(m) I can name or describe most of the shapes on the sheet.		
I listen carefully to my partner's instructions so I know which shape they want me to put a counter on.		
I try to give a clear description of a shape to my partner.		

Name _____

Lesson 27: Compass directions	I think	My partner thinks
(m) I can accurately use compass directions.		
(☒) I listen to the route instructions my partner gives me.		
(☺) I worked hard today.		

Lesson 28: Coordinates	I think	My partner thinks
(m) I can describe the position of a square, using coordinates.		
(☒) I discuss with my partner what questions to ask in the game.		
(☺) I work with my partner to complete the task we have been set.		

Self and peer assessment

Resource sheets

RS1

1	2	3	4	5	6	7
8	9	10	11	12	13	14
15	16	17	18	19	20	21
22	23	24	25	26	27	28
29	30	31	32	33	34	35
36	37	38	39	40	41	42
43	44	45	46	47	48	49

1	2	3	4	5	6	7
8	9	10	11	12	13	14
15	16	17	18	19	20	21
22	23	24	25	26	27	28
29	30	31	32	33	34	35
36	37	38	39	40	41	42
43	44	45	46	47	48	49

Maths Out Loud *Year 3*   Lesson 1

RS2

Is the mystery number odd?	Is the mystery number even?
Is the mystery number greater than 20?	Is the mystery number greater than _____?
Is the mystery number less than 15?	Is the mystery number less than _____?
Does the mystery number end in 4?	Does the mystery number end in _____?
Does the mystery number have a 7 in it?	Does the mystery number have a _____ in it?
Is the mystery number greater than _____?	Is the mystery number greater than 5?
Is the mystery number less than _____?	Is the mystery number less than 20?
Does the mystery number end in _____?	Does the mystery number end in 2?
Is the mystery number in the 4 times table?	Is the mystery number in the _____ times table?
Does the mystery number have a _____ in it?	Does the mystery number have a _____ in it?
Is the mystery number a multiple of _____?	Is the mystery number a multiple of 6?
Is the mystery number in the 3 times table?	Is the mystery number in the _____ times table?
Is the mystery number a multiple of 5?	Is the mystery number a multiple of _____?

Maths Out Loud *Year 3*   Lesson 1

Name _____   RS3

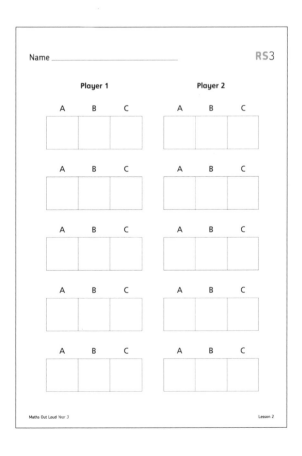

Maths Out Loud *Year 3*   Lesson 2

Name _____   RS4

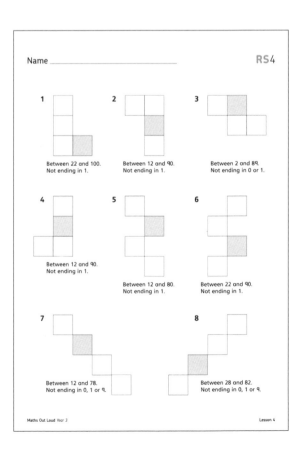

1 Between 22 and 100. Not ending in 1.

2 Between 12 and 90. Not ending in 1.

3 Between 2 and 89. Not ending in 0 or 1.

4 Between 12 and 90. Not ending in 1.

5 Between 12 and 80. Not ending in 1.

6 Between 22 and 90. Not ending in 1.

7 Between 12 and 78. Not ending in 0, 1 or 9.

8 Between 28 and 82. Not ending in 0, 1 or 9.

Maths Out Loud *Year 3*   Lesson 4

RS5

Name _____

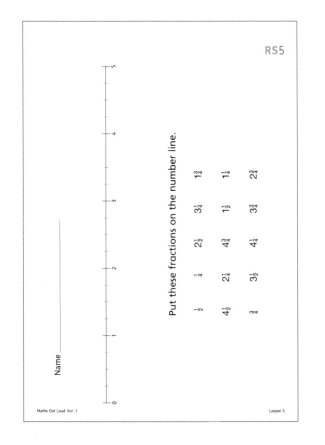

Put these fractions on the number line.

$\frac{1}{2}$ $\frac{1}{4}$ $2\frac{1}{2}$ $3\frac{1}{4}$ $1\frac{3}{4}$

$4\frac{1}{2}$ $2\frac{1}{4}$ $4\frac{3}{4}$ $1\frac{1}{2}$ $1\frac{1}{4}$

$\frac{3}{4}$ $3\frac{1}{2}$ $4\frac{1}{4}$ $3\frac{3}{4}$ $2\frac{3}{4}$

Maths Out Loud Year 3   Lesson 5

RS6

Name _____

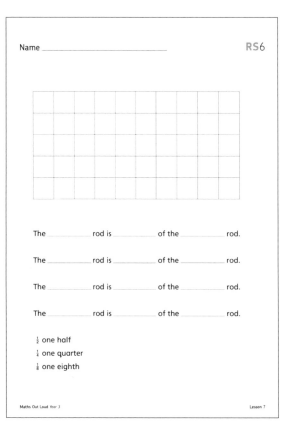

The _____ rod is _____ of the _____ rod.

The _____ rod is _____ of the _____ rod.

The _____ rod is _____ of the _____ rod.

The _____ rod is _____ of the _____ rod.

$\frac{1}{2}$ one half

$\frac{1}{4}$ one quarter

$\frac{1}{8}$ one eighth

Maths Out Loud Year 3   Lesson 7

RS7

10 beads $\frac{1}{2}$ green	12 beads $\frac{1}{2}$ red	16 beads $\frac{1}{2}$ blue
12 beads $\frac{1}{4}$ yellow	12 beads $\frac{1}{4}$ blue	12 beads $\frac{1}{4}$ green
16 beads $\frac{3}{4}$ red	16 beads $\frac{3}{4}$ yellow	16 beads $\frac{3}{4}$ green
20 beads $\frac{1}{8}$ yellow	20 beads $\frac{1}{8}$ red	20 beads $\frac{1}{8}$ blue
12 beads $\frac{1}{2}$ blue $\frac{1}{2}$ red	16 beads $\frac{1}{4}$ yellow $\frac{1}{4}$ green	20 beads $\frac{3}{4}$ red $\frac{1}{8}$ blue

Maths Out Loud Year 3   Lesson 8

RS8

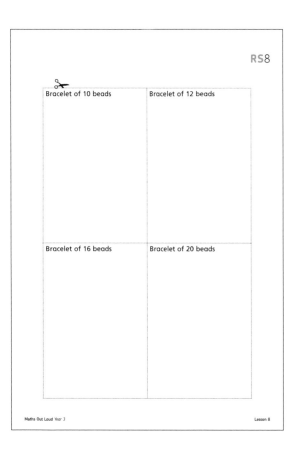

Bracelet of 10 beads	Bracelet of 12 beads
Bracelet of 16 beads	Bracelet of 20 beads

Maths Out Loud Year 3   Lesson 8

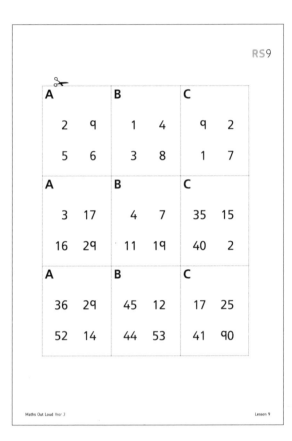

RS9

A	B	C
2 9	1 4	9 2
5 6	3 8	1 7

A	B	C
3 17	4 7	35 15
16 29	11 19	40 2

A	B	C
36 29	45 12	17 25
52 14	44 53	41 90

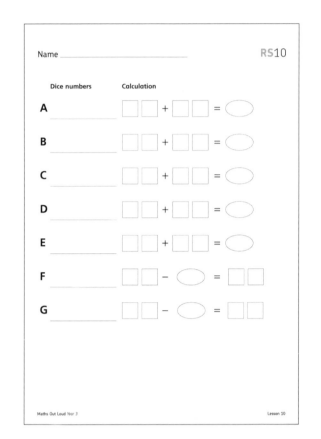

Name _____

RS10

Dice numbers   Calculation

A _____ ☐☐ + ☐☐ = ◯

B _____ ☐☐ + ☐☐ = ◯

C _____ ☐☐ + ☐☐ = ◯

D _____ ☐☐ + ☐☐ = ◯

E _____ ☐☐ + ☐☐ = ◯

F _____ ☐☐ – ◯ = ☐☐

G _____ ☐☐ – ◯ = ☐☐

RS11

13	25	5	10	30	19
40	9	32	12	50	250
20	15	11	21	22	85
60	100	45	16	35	34
43	32	65	300	17	4
37	29	150	70	95	54

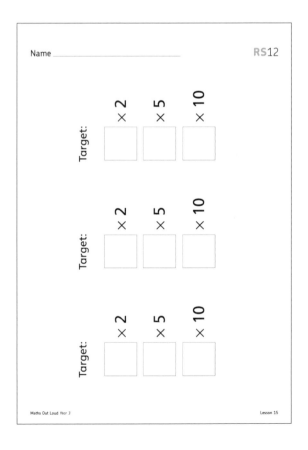

Name _____

RS12

Target: × 2 ☐ × 5 ☐ × 10 ☐

Target: × 2 ☐ × 5 ☐ × 10 ☐

Target: × 2 ☐ × 5 ☐ × 10 ☐

Name _____ RS13

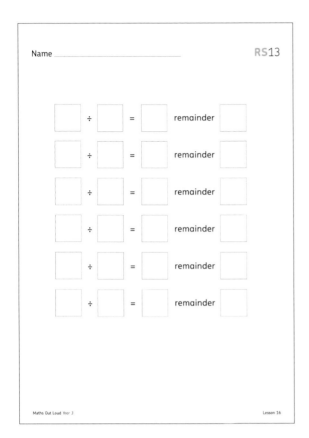

	÷		=		remainder	

Name _____ RS14

Number you are dividing by

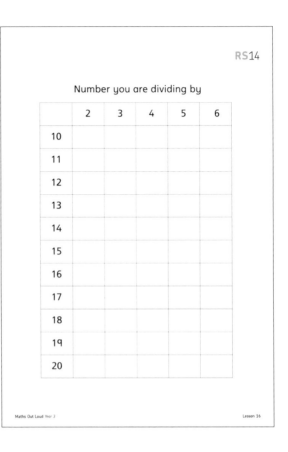

	2	3	4	5	6
10					
11					
12					
13					
14					
15					
16					
17					
18					
19					
20					

Name _____ RS15

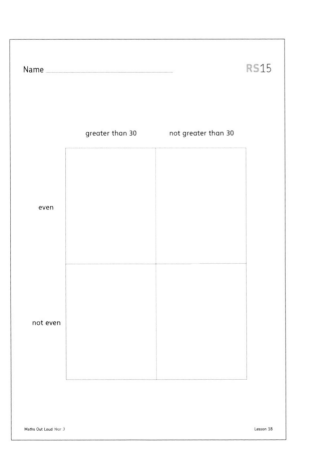

	greater than 30	not greater than 30
even		
not even		

Name _____ RS16

Names containing the letter _____

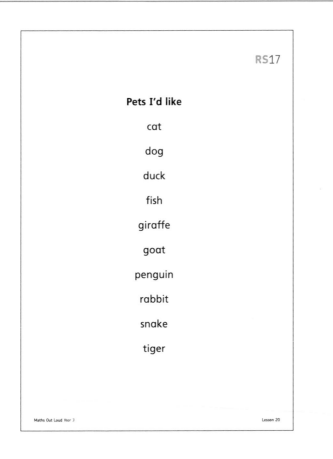

RS17

Pets I'd like

cat

dog

duck

fish

giraffe

goat

penguin

rabbit

snake

tiger

Maths Out Loud *Year 3*   Lesson 20

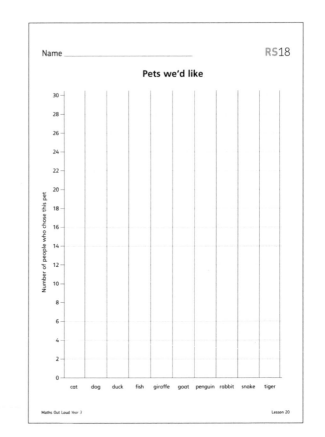

Name _____   RS18

Pets we'd like

Maths Out Loud *Year 3*   Lesson 20

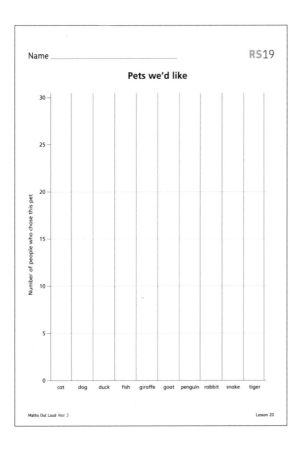

Name _____   RS19

Pets we'd like

Maths Out Loud *Year 3*   Lesson 20

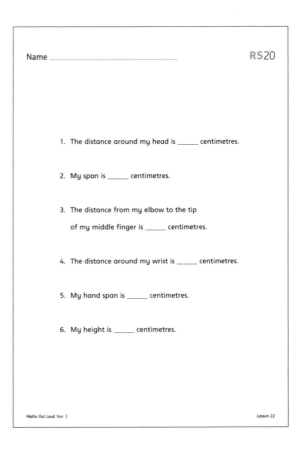

Name _____   RS20

1. The distance around my head is _____ centimetres.

2. My span is _____ centimetres.

3. The distance from my elbow to the tip
   of my middle finger is _____ centimetres.

4. The distance around my wrist is _____ centimetres.

5. My hand span is _____ centimetres.

6. My height is _____ centimetres.

Maths Out Loud *Year 3*   Lesson 22

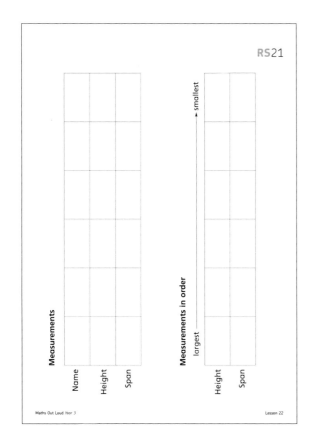

RS21

Measurements

Name		
Height		
Span		

Measurements in order

largest → smallest

| Height | |
| Span | |

Maths Out Loud Year 3

Lesson 22

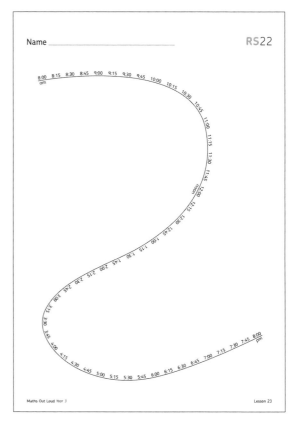

Name _____

RS22

8:00 am 8:15 8:30 8:45 9:00 9:15 9:30 9:45 10:00 10:15 10:30 10:45 11:00 11:15 11:30 11:45 noon 12:15 12:30 12:45 1:00 1:15 1:30 1:45 2:00 2:15 2:30 2:45 3:00 3:15 3:30 3:45 4:00 4:15 4:30 4:45 5:00 5:15 5:30 5:45 6:00 6:15 6:30 6:45 7:00 7:15 7:30 7:45 8:00 pm

Maths Out Loud Year 3

Lesson 23

RS23

30 minutes	half an hour	15 minutes	quarter of an hour
45 minutes	three quarters of an hour	60 minutes	1 hour
30 minutes	half an hour	15 minutes	quarter of an hour
45 minutes	three quarters of an hour	60 minutes	1 hour
30 minutes	half an hour	15 minutes	quarter of an hour
45 minutes	three quarters of an hour	60 minutes	1 hour

Maths Out Loud Year 3

Lesson 23

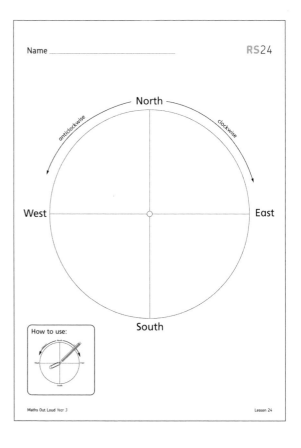

Name _____

RS24

North

anticlockwise

clockwise

West

East

South

How to use:

Maths Out Loud Year 3

Lesson 24

RS25

$\frac{1}{4}$ turn clockwise	$\frac{1}{4}$ turn clockwise	2 right-angled turns clockwise	2 right-angled turns clockwise
$\frac{1}{4}$ turn anticlockwise	$\frac{1}{4}$ turn anticlockwise	2 right-angled turns anticlockwise	2 right-angled turns anticlockwise
$\frac{1}{4}$ turn clockwise	$\frac{1}{4}$ turn clockwise	1 right-angled turn clockwise	1 right-angled turn clockwise
$\frac{1}{4}$ turn anticlockwise	$\frac{1}{4}$ turn anticlockwise	1 right-angled turn anticlockwise	1 right-angled turn anticlockwise
$\frac{1}{4}$ turn clockwise	$\frac{1}{4}$ turn clockwise	3 right-angled turns clockwise	3 right-angled turns clockwise
$\frac{1}{4}$ turn anticlockwise	$\frac{1}{4}$ turn anticlockwise	3 right-angled turns anticlockwise	3 right-angled turns anticlockwise

Maths Out Loud *Year 3* Lesson 24

RS26

Name _____

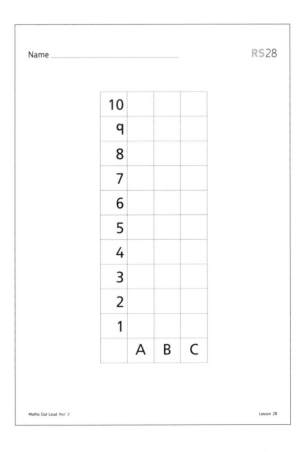

Maths Out Loud *Year 3* Lesson 26

RS27

Name _____

North
West ← → East
South

A	B	C	D	E	F	G	H
.	a	b	c	d	e	f	I
–	g	h	i	j	k	l	J
Z	m	n	o	p	q	r	K
Y	s	t	u	v	w	x	L
X	y	z	a	e	i	o	M
W	u	y	l	m	r	n	N
V	U	T	S	R	Q	P	O

Maths Out Loud *Year 3* Lesson 27

RS28

Name _____

10			
9			
8			
7			
6			
5			
4			
3			
2			
1			
	A	B	C

Maths Out Loud *Year 3* Lesson 28

Name _____

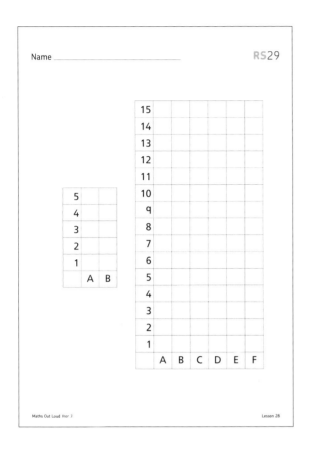